The Show that Wouldn't Die

Bryan Johnston

This book is dedicated to Soren and Tova.
Because they are amazing.

"I got the best job in the city. And I honestly felt that, I felt that this was the greatest job in this whole city. I can't imagine somebody who had a better job than I did."
John Keister

"We were living the life."
Ross Shafer

"What I miss most is waking up every day knowing that I get to spend the entire day playing with my best friends."
Nancy Guppy

"It was amazing that I was on the show for ten years. I felt like I got away with something."
Bob Nelson

"I still feel very lucky they kept me around."
Bill Nye

"I was thinking, I can't believe I'm barely getting paid for this."
Joe Guppy

"It was the most fun you'll ever have in your life in terms of a job."
Tracey Conway

"It was very much like a kid's summer camp comedy thing but it reached this incredibly high level so it was this really bizarre scenario."
Ed Wyatt

"The beauty of it was, nobody told you what to do, you needed to do your own thing, and that sort of sustained on the show."
Pat Cashman

"I didn't realize how being on that show changed the course of everything for me."
Lauren Weedman

"I kept saying over and over to people, 'You don't realize what a gift this is and how great it is, and when this is over you'll realize it.'"
Steve Wilson

"It was the time of my life."
Joel McHale

Table of Contents

1. Forward   7

2. Who's who   13

3. In the beginning…   23

4. Along comes John   35

5. The early years   45

6. Bill Nye the Science Guy   57

7. Louie Louie   63

8. The lure of LA   67

9. Ross gets his wish   71

10. The changing of the guard   75

11. A new beginning   81

12. Coming and going   89

13. The prank that failed (April Fools)   93

14. Speaking of getting in trouble   101

15. Seattle in the spotlight   109

16. Seattle music scene sidebar   113

17. The return of Ms. Guppy   121

18. Facetime   127

19. Bye, bye, Bill Nye   131

20. Comedy Central   135

21. Dying is easy, comedy is hard   139

22. How do they come up with this stuff?   145

23. The Secret of their success   181

24. Recognition has its perks   195

25. The newbies   203

26. This is the end   213

The Players 🎭

Ross Shafer—Host

John Keister—Host, cast member

Bill Stainton—Producer, cast member

Pat Cashman—Cast member

Bill Nye—Cast member

Steve Wilson—Director, cast member

Joe Guppy—Cast member

Nancy Guppy—Cast member

Tracey Conway—Cast member

Ed Wyatt—Cast member

Bob Nelson—Cast member

Lauren Weedman—Cast member

Joel McHale—Cast member

Andrea "Andy" Stein—Cast member

Matt Smith—Cast member

Dana Dwinell—Producer

Mike Neun—Show writer

Jim Sharp—Show writer

Scott Schaefer—Show writer

Jim McKenna—Associate producer

Hans-Eric Gosch—Associate producer

Ralph Bevins—Shooter, editor

Darrell Suto—Shooter, editor, Billy Quan

Jay Cascio—KING-TV VP of Programming

Rick Blangiardi—KING-TV General Manager

Jeff Gilbert—Rocket magazine music editor

Joleen Winther Hughes—Music promoter, Manager RCKCNDY

Dave Krieg—Seattle Seahawks Quarterback

Jim Zorn—Seattle Seahawks Quarterback

Dave Wyman—Seattle Seahawks Linebacker, Radio Host

Dori Monson—Radio host

Marty Riemer—Radio host

Feliks Banel—Media historian

John Findlay—Professor of History

Pepper Schwartz—Professor of Sociology

Norm Rice—Seattle Mayor

Kim Thayil—Lead guitarist, Soundgarden

Chris Ballew—Lead Singer, The Presidents of the United States of America

Dan Lewis—KOMO-TV Anchor

Steve Raible—KIRO-TV Anchor

Tony Ventrella—KING-TV Sports Director

Jeff Renner—KING-TV Chief Meteorologist

Erik Lacitis—Seattle Times columnist

Almost Live

Forward

I find it astonishing that it took almost two thousand years after the birth of Christ for someone to take serious comic aim at Speed Walking. I mean, honestly, how is that even possible? Speed Walking looks so patently ridiculous you would think the laff wastelands would be littered with gags. But no. It took a two-bit sketch comedy show in a forgotten corner of the country to send up Speed Walking to the level it so richly deserves. But that is the way of Almost Live! They had a knack for finding the funny in areas where we watch and think, Duh, of course they're making fun of that. But as was so often the case, no one else had before. The sketches were remarkably fresh and original. Especially to locals. Out-of-towners could sense the gags were funny; I mean, funny writing is still funny writing, but since they didn't get the inside-jokiness, many of the bits didn't have the same zing. The absurdity of cops busting a guy for trying to pass off tap water as Evian water is cute, but the fact that the guy had the temerity to do so on Mercer Island where it's illegal to drink anything as bourgeois as tap water takes it to another level. Someone from Chicago wouldn't get that jokes about Kenny G are extra funny around here. In Dallas they have no idea how spot-on *Dating a Boeing Engineer* really is. Time and again you would try to explain the funny to your friend who just moved here and in the end just shake your head and say, "It's a Northwest thing." And you said it with no small measure of pride. It's kind of our own secret club. I can't help but think it's what redheads and left-handers feel. You take pride where you can get it.

For many of the cast and crew the show was a launching pad to national recognition and fame. But no one saw it coming. Its success was absolutely ninja-like. In the early years I can promise you not a soul would have bet their mortgage on the show's longevity. Most every season was treated like Westley by the

Dread Pirate Roberts in The Princess Bride: "Good night, Westley. Good job. Sleep well. I'll most likely kill you in the morning."

And yet they kept coming back, and for the least sexy reason imaginable: They were good. Hey, talent is talent, funny is funny. Go to YouTube and watch *Roscoe's Rug Emporium* and I dare you not to smile. After a while we took the show for granted. We tuned in expecting it to be funny, because it had trained us to that mind-set. When a bit fell flat it actually pissed us off a little because, dammit, they're usually funny! But we cut them slack because they were our home team. We loved the fact that our own little homegrown comedy show was quality merchandise. This was robin's egg blue Tiffany box funny, not "authentic" Rolex out of your cousin Vinny's trunk funny. This was the good stuff. And it was ours!

So many of the sketches are burned into our memories. *High-Five'n White Guys. Worst Girlfriend in the World. Ineffectual Middle-Management Suck Ups. Sluggy.* You still get a laugh reminiscing about them at parties. You find yourself singing along to *Folk Songs of South King County (Kisses sweeter than Schlitz, Kegger in the field,* and that classic *I'm going to sit right down and drink beer 'til I pass out).* The jokes were actually clever and had wit, and whether we want to admit it or not were pretty spot-on (see above folk songs).

Billy Quan bits were funny like Beyonce is cute. Cops in Kent / Ballard / Wallingford / Mercer Island / Leavenworth / Redmond / U-District were Elvis good. Before Vegas and the silly clothes. And the sketches actually had something Saturday Night Live sketches didn't: endings. I know, crazy, right? The sketches wrapped up nice and tight instead of simply stumbling along until the producer hit the "applause" sign to cue the audience that the bit was over. Watching SNL drove me nuts. I'd watch, grinding my teeth, yelling at the TV, "Give me an ending, damn you!"

Almost Live! had the goods, but talent is no guarantee of success in television. It takes a healthy dose of timing, faith and luck to stick around, and for reasons too many to count the planets all happened to line up in their favor. For starters Almost Live! aired on KING 5, a remarkably patient television station with local ownership that wasn't afraid to take a few chances. In the beginning the cast and crew were given the opportunity to figure things out, to step on a few upturned rakes while they found their footing. Unlike the financial sword of Damocles hanging over new shows today it wasn't a case of deliver instant ratings or else. In the mid-'80s, when cable was still young, most people didn't have a million channels to choose from. People wanted their MTV but only 40% were wired for it. For more than half the viewing audience it was the Networks or nothing. Almost Live! was blessed with an audience that, for the most part, had to choose between chocolate, vanilla and strawberry.

That's not to say everything fell in their lap. Almost Live! was given a pretty long leash but the long leash had a tight collar. The station spent virtually nothing on the show. Need a prop? Build it in the basement. Need professional actors for a sketch? Find a warm body in the sales department to play the role. Full-blown marketing and promotional campaigns? Heh, heh, that's cute.

Keeping in line with countless other success story the show was populated with true believers and countered roadblocks and potholes with the infamously stubborn Screw You defense. Local comedy can't work on TV? Screw you; we think it can. Need national talent to make it work? Screw you; we've got all the talent we need right here.

Almost Live! is a tale of survival; it had a ridiculously long lifespan. Fifteen years, not including reruns which have been running non-stop ever since. You're thinking, Wait, fifteen years? That can't be right! There's no way that show aired for that long!

But it did. A child born in its first season was a high school freshman in its last. During its run President Reagan handed over the Oval Office keys to George W. Bush who passed them along to Bill Clinton. In that same window of time the Internet rose, the Berlin wall fell and Grunge music was born (and to many, died). Almost Live! survived a massive schedule and format change, two things that would normally deep-six a show. It lost its host, got a new one. Survived. It pulled a prank that ended up on the front page of every paper in America and nearly got the show cancelled. Survived. It aired a sketch that almost got the entire cast fired. Survived. One of the cast members literally died on stage. Survived.

For fifteen years, hundreds of thousands of people throughout the region woke every morning to drive rivets, write code, brew coffee or compose actuarial tables, while a handful of lucky-pucks on Dexter Avenue had the great good fortune to spend their waking hours cracking wise and taking jabs at Northwest culture. For a living, damn them. For what the rest of us did over beers with our pals these blessed few were getting paychecks. Usually tiny paychecks but cashable nonetheless. They were handed the keys to the candy shop—a shop with no surveillance cameras, mind you—and ran rampant. Think about that. They had virtually no oversight, other than common sense, which occasionally betrayed them. They created what they wanted to create. They didn't have to run their ideas (95% of the time) past management. On one occasion they did and it probably saved them their jobs. On another occasion they didn't and it almost cost them their jobs. They didn't have to deal with the bane of all creatives— focus groups—they got to trust their instincts; they didn't make decisions based on research, they went on gut feeling. For fifteen years they got to run with scissors, jump on the bed and eat dessert before dinner. Think about that the next time your pointy-haired boss asks if the client proposal you worked on over the weekend has the appropriate *synergy*.

The show was so very Seattle. Even the weekly pitch meetings, where sketches and jokes were first introduced, were generally polite and supportive; a far cry from the infamous Saturday Night Live pitch meeting blood baths. Everyone wanted their stuff on the air but was still happy to see each other succeed. There really was no 'I' in this team.

They unapologetically traded on local stereotypes. Ballard is filled with old Norwegians who are crappy drivers. Ya, sure, youbetcha. In Kent women's hair must be teased out at least 20 inches and all males under 35 years of age must wear caps. No kidding. Everyone confuses Pike and Pine. I see you nodding your head. The show painted in broad strokes but a newcomer could still divine more about the region from watching a few episodes than wading through a Seattle tourism welcome kit.

At the show's peak the cast members took on cult status in Seattle. They were anointed local celebrities, which are few and far between in this region. But during the show's heyday their level of celebrity was of the more everyman variety. People had no fear of chatting them up, offering praise or busting their chops in equal measure. They could find themselves confronted by gang members, as one does, and end up trading witty banter with them. Yes, that did happen.

And speaking of the cast, they were a who's who of unexpected success: A bald guy with a funny name and questionable interview skills becomes the ringleader and local hero. A mad scientist with a thing for liquid nitrogen becomes one of the show's breakout stars and later, a national celebrity. A quiet, reserved writer eventually finds his name on the Academy Awards® ballot. One of the station's promotion producers becomes the show's comedy Sybil, morphing into countless roles. A nine-to-fiver in the station's HR department becomes the show's preeminent 'actor'. A fearless comedic couple finds fame in LA, nearly at the cost of their marriage. And an intern makes the leap to legitimate Hollywood star.

Almost Live! was the perfect show at the perfect time in the perfect place. The show grew up at precisely the same time Seattle did. During Almost Live!'s lifespan Seattle went from the quiet bookish girl to the smoking hot one everyone wants to date: Miss Congeniality to Miss America. The area was suddenly cool enough to be made fun of. But ironically the city's invitation to the cool kid's table was arguably a factor in the show's ultimate demise. The show was a perfect mirror to the region. It was topical, it was relevant, it was unique. But popularity has its price. As the national spotlight fried the corneas of the Northwest, Seattle's uniqueness was slowly sanded off with 80-grit. The region homogenized, local flavor was lost and everything began to taste a bit like chicken. Community stereotypes weren't quite so stereotypish. Stage one cancer to funny.

This is a book of memories, some a bit faded with time. I interviewed a lot of people for this book and not all the memories lined up perfectly. Not surprising. Most of us forget where we left our car keys this morning let alone what we were doing three decades ago. I did my best to get confirmation on the facts and cross-referenced people's recollections. I tried to offer both sides of any conflicts. Most people I reached out to responded and gladly gave their side. Some didn't. I think I've got consensus for the most part. However there are still a couple of events that are recalled quite differently. Like, not even in the same zip code. All I can do is present to you what each person recalls and let the chips fall where they may. This is their story told from their perspective.

Enjoy your time in the Way-Back machine.

Ask a parent to go all Sophie's Choice and pick their favorite child and they won't do it. They suddenly become the world's greatest politicians, incapable of favoritism. John Keister and Bill Stainton were, for all intents and purposes, Almost Live!'s parents. Well, adopted parents. Legal guardians, perhaps. John was on the show for the entire run while Bill Stainton was the producer for 13 of the 15 years. They worked with every single cast and crewmember. Who better to ask to get a quick glimpse, a Reader's Digest summary, of all the main players?

About Ross Shafer

(Bill Stainton)

- Ross Shafer, Mr. Smooth, I mean he was a really good host. He was born to be a host; he had the hair for it. When we would have our pitch meetings everyone would have one or two ideas and he would have ten. He worked his ass off; he took it very, very seriously. He was really good at monologues.

(John Keister)

- There wouldn't have been a show without Ross. People tend to underestimate what a good interviewer and solid host he was. He's also one of the funniest people I've ever met – when he was offstage. He would tone down his comedy during the show, I think because he didn't want to offend the audience. He was a little hard on me at the very beginning but once I proved that I could get laughs and make the show better he got behind me 100 percent. I would have never become the host if Ross hadn't established the show and let me do my style of comedy. We worked well as a team and he was very disappointed when I didn't join him in LA on the Late Show. He went through the show business blender down there and I'm very happy at how successful he has become on the speaking circuit. I'm not surprised by his success, that guy never let anything get him down.

Pat Cashman

(Bill Stainton)

- Pat Cashman was our Phil Hartman, he's good looking and he can do anything. He could do broad comedy he could do smart comedy and he was prolific, he came up with lots and lots of ideas.

(John Keister)

- I learned more from Pat than anyone else in the business. He was like a father figure to me and I constantly sought his approval. He understood the power that silence has in comedy. He could do more with a well-timed pause than any comedian I've ever seen. He was always busy—doing radio, commercials, editing. He was loved by everybody in the building yet he was a bit of a lone wolf and he definitely made his own rules.

Bill Nye

(Bill Stainton)

- Bill Nye was our version of the wacky neighbor. He thought differently than the rest of us. So he would come up with these ideas that no one else would come up with. I think that came from the fact that he came from a different world; he came from the world of science and engineering. So he literally saw the world differently from those of us who came from the world of comedy or TV.

(John Keister)

- Tremendous performer and a very nice person. His writing was a little weird. At the writers meetings we used to call his submissions "Jokes of the Future". His success is truly worldwide, which I know he is proud of. I've never known anyone who was less aware of how he was being perceived by other people, which led to some truly bizarre moments.

Joe Guppy

(Bill Stainton)

- Joe Guppy was fearless. He would do anything. He was an actor's actor. He would do stuff and I would be like, How can you do that? I would be so embarrassed. And he would come up with these amazingly offbeat ideas. He was such an artist, and I mean that in every sense, he took his writing so seriously.

(John Keister)

- Joe created "Speed Walker" but knew that Nye should be the character. I need to say that up front because back in the day Joe was very concerned about getting the proper credit. We had a similar sense of what was funny which was deemed a little "too hip" in the early days of the show. It was easier for me to get material on the air so Joe frequently wrote and performed in bits with just the two of us. He was very ambitious and managed to get to Hollywood quickly. It was there that he decided on a radical change in careers. As he said to me, he had to go to the craziest city in the world to get sane. He's a great therapist and has helped thousands of people through his practice.

Nancy Guppy

(Bill Stainton)

- Nancy Guppy, extremely versatile. She could pull off just about anything. One of our go-to people. There's a real passion in Nancy.

(John Keister)

- I love talking to Nancy. I see her more often than any other member of the cast. She would get pissed off in ways that I thought were hilarious. For one bit she was dressed as a hooker on Aurora. Guys pulled over, she screamed at them, and was mad for an hour. She used to channel that anger into sketches like one where I was looking at a model in a magazine and Nancy, playing my wife, started stabbing the photo and vowed to track the woman down and kill her. She brings the same intensity to her show on the Seattle channel.

Bob Nelson

(Bill Stainton)

- Bob Nelson was the most brilliant comedy writer I've ever known. When he first sent me his sample material it was brilliant. There were sketches, there were jokes, there were ideas for bits. Brilliant, brilliant writer.

(John Keister)

- I believe I'm one of the few people on the planet that has witnessed Bob fly into an obscenity-laced, throwing things around the room, fit of rage. It was so unusual that the object of his anger had to ask me if it was real or not. I assured him that it was. I only bring this up because I'm sure that everybody else is saying that he's the nicest person in the world (which he is). Best writer I've ever worked with. His only vice is dessert.

Ed Wyatt

(Bill Stainton)

- Ed Wyatt offered a real fresh look at things. He was really good at doing what are called interstitials, which were these little things we did coming out of breaks or going into breaks. These little quirky bits that ran around 15 seconds and he was great at coming up with things like that. Plus women really loved Ed Wyatt. Could be the raspy voice, I don't know.

(John Keister)
- Ed gave me my first shot of Jägermeister. He had a lot of great comedy ideas and played some wonderful characters but anybody who knows Ed realizes that his overriding passion is for sports. He also loves to travel the world. He's down in Australia now as a sports commentator—it seems like the world really worked out for him.

Tracey Conway

(Bill Stainton)

- Tracey Conway, consummate actress. She was the only one with an acting degree. I think she had an MFA from USC. Ally Sheedy was one of her classmates. So conscientious of her craft. You could throw anything at her and she could do it.

(John Keister)
- Tracey worked as an administrative assistant in the Human Resources department at KING. I think she had just about given up on her dreams of being an actor, but now she's had a bigger and longer career than almost anyone else in her Master of Fine Arts graduating class at USC. We started using her in parts and gradually she was doing more work on the show than in Human Relations so she officially joined the cast. She had a very sweet personality but loved playing bad girls like "The Worst Girlfriend in the World". You could always depend on Tracey. Not even a cardiac arrest could stop her. Best legs in the business.

Steve Wilson

(Bill Stainton)

- Steve Wilson, as a director, he got the show. He and I had battles, I think anyone will tell you I don't think there was anyone who did not have an in your face, horrible fight with Steve, he was very volatile. But I wouldn't want to have anyone else in the director's booth.

(John Keister)

- Steve knew where everything was and how everything really worked at KING. He was like the old guy in the hardware store who could tell you exactly what you needed right as you walked through the door. Great director. He also was the most social of the group, throwing lavish parties and participating in meetings and events that the rest of us avoided. He screamed a bit more than I thought necessary but the show always came out right on time.

Joel McHale

(Bill Stainton)

- Joel McHale, amazingly talented, he brought youth to the show. When we first started the show we were all in our twenties. All of a sudden we're in our late thirties and forties and it's really sort of a young person's sport and Joel McHale brought that. He brought that youth, he brought that vitality. I wish we could have had him with us longer. Whatever happened to him anyway? I hope he landed on his feet.

(John Keister)

- I met Joel on a movie set when he was still at the UW and I recommended him for an intern position. He was an extremely polite and effective intern and became a great cast member. Things were written for him that played up his leading man good looks but he had a line that he refused to cross. He didn't like to participate in sketches that hinted at immorality or certain sexual situations. I'm talking about very tame stuff here but he was a real moral church-going young man. We used to say he'd never make it in Hollywood if he stuck to those views. Guess we were wrong about that. I remember him as a happy, nice, athletic young man who displayed none of the snark that seems to define his presence on TV today.

Lauren Weedman

(Bill Stainton)

- Lauren Weedman had a quirkiness that made me a little uncomfortable, but John loved it, but it was cool that she brought that to the show, that little bit of discomfort. Really, really funny, but never fit in but was brilliant, that was kind of Lauren.

(John Keister)

- Amazing performer – with no filter. She would say anything to anyone. Being on the show didn't seem particularly important to her. When she made it to the Daily Show with John Stewart I called her and asked if she was at least pretending that she liked it there. Her response was, "Oh my God, did they call you?" I saw her do things on stage that literally took my breath away.

Bill Stainton

(John Keister)

- The most important thing about Bill is that he deeply understands comedy, which I've discovered is very rare with producers. The original producer of the show didn't like what she called "mean comedy" which I came to realize was anything with an edge to it. When she left we were all nervous about who was going to replace her. We were really lucky to get Bill as our producer.

John Keister

(Bill Stainton)

- John Keister was so unique. He had the edge, he had the attitude, which was crucial to me, and his strong, strong, strong Seattle roots. More so than anyone else on the show. John loved Seattle and Seattle history.

Almost Live

1984

- Final Four in Seattle.
- USSR boycotts the Olympic games in LA.
- Seahawks retire the number 12 jersey. The 12's are officially born.
- The first commercial CD players are introduced.
- Band Aid performs "Do they know it's Christmas?" to raise money for Ethiopia famine relief.

In the Beginning...

It all started with a man named Bob Jones. He was KING-TV's Program Director and he was on a mission. The year was 1984.

(Jim McKenna) I was a floor director/stage manager, I'd been working in sports television and we had a new Program Director named Bob Jones, and we were kind of terrified of this guy because he was this hot shot who'd come in and a lot of times everyone gets fired when a new Program Director comes in. But I remember hearing that he wanted a show that he kept saying would be like Dean Martin and the Gold Diggers [sic]. A comedy/variety show out of the Pacific Northwest. He'd say stuff like, "We can do a show from the ferry; we can do a show from the Space Needle!"

(Pat Cashman) He was one of those guys that really loved this idea of doing local shows, and KING was said to be the most prolific producer of local programing of any station in the county, except one in Boston, I believe.

(Steve Wilson) They wanted to grow a show that could be done as a strip, five nights a week.

(Jim McKenna) I'd had a dream of working in comedy television since 1975 when I started at KING and I was actually working in radio and they got me a gig as a page for the Seattle Today show, and I was going to quit because TV was so F-ing boring at that time and I wanted to go back into rock and roll radio. Then one night I'm at a college party, the party stops, the kids say, "You gotta see this show, it's the funniest damn thing you'll ever see"— and I remember John Belushi coming up in a bee suit. The light bulb went off and I thought this is the funniest thing I've ever seen, maybe I'll stay in TV and maybe I'll get to do something fun like that. So I kept my head down, just trying not to get fired.

(John Keister) Bob Jones had all these ideas about lots of different shows that he wanted to try and get going and they were trying different hosts; David Silverman was a host, there was some guy, they flew him from I believe Washington DC, but it wasn't quite happening.

(Dana Dwinell) The initial pilots did not go well.

(Jim McKenna) They had the two failed pilots; I think there was a show called Take Five and another called Rain City Gazette.

(John Keister) Rainy Day Gazette, I believe was it.

(Steve Wilson) I was in the meetings for the planning of these shows. We did a couple of pilots and then my suggestion was, there was this brand new show that came on called Late Night with David Letterman, it's like a hipped up version of the Tonight

Show. It's got a really rocking band, and he's really cool. Let's do our own David Letterman show, a local version.

(Ross Shafer) That could not be more false. [Steve] wasn't associated with our show in the first year, our director was Mark Warner and Mark was a seasoned guy who came in and really taught us about television. I don't think Wilson was around– certainly was not around when they were creating the show, was not around when we were launching the ideas or my conversations with Bob Jones or Pat Cashman.

(Steve Wilson) It was my suggestion that we should do a David Letterman show. Ross came in and had his own writers, he had Jim Sharp and he brought Mike [Neun], but as far as the TV part goes he wasn't even part of that. I worked at the TV station. I was a producer/director here. It was my job to come up with new programming and then produce it. We have a production department, we had a Program Director who wanted to do this access show that would come on five nights a week so we did several pilots and the one that we did with Ross was the one where I said, "You know what, here's what I think we should do, we should do a copy of the Letterman show. We should have a band, we should have a host and we should do this." That's my story and I'm sticking to it.

(Ross Shafer) From 1976 - '80 I had my own series of small businesses. Two stereo/pet shops, a T-shirt imprint store, sandwich café, ice cream parlor and photo portrait studio. I did Community Theater but I got burned out working 24/7/365 so I took the job as Advertising Director of the Squire Shops in 1980. That was a pretty big job for me but I was unhappy there and they had asked me to fudge my reports so they could get more advertising money and I couldn't do it. My best friend at the time was Chip Hanauer who was the Personnel Director there as well as driving their boat (Miss Squire Shop). In '81 Jim Sharp and I opened our own advertising agency, which was pretty successful, while I still did stand up comedy. It was in '83 that I won the Seattle International Comedy Competition...[and suddenly] I was in demand. I was able to work as the opening act for singers like Dionne Warwick and Eddie Rabbitt, Crystal Gayle; I was kind of living my dream at that time.

(John Keister) I believe [Ross] was recommended by Pat Cashman because Pat had seen him on a local, I think on a show in Canada. We used to watch Canadian TV, the cable system [carried the

channels] and he was on some show and Pat thought, You know, this guy seems to be very poised. He is not killing, he is not doing great, but it's not getting to him—which is an important thing, and especially for somebody who is going to be hosting a show.

(Pat Cashman) I saw him on a talk show in Vancouver I think it was, and I thought that this guy is really good, very articulate and smooth, and a local guy. So I went to Bob Jones.

(Ross Shafer) They had already done a pilot and I can't remember what it was called but a friend of mine, David Silverman, was also a comedian who did the pilot and for some reason it didn't test as well as they thought it would and so Bob Jones called me in and said, "Would you be interested in doing a television show?" At that time, I had a manger and an agent and my question rather had been, "Yes, but how much does it pay?" I had no interest in it and I think he said it was $500 and I went to my agent and said, "I can't take a cut in pay to do a TV show." I was making pretty good money at the time. My manager John Powell was with me, and he said, "You better rethink this, this could be really important for you." So I took his advice, then Bob said, "Have you produced a TV show before?" and I lied to him, I said, "I have been around television a lot and yes, I could do that." So, then he said, "We want to shoot a pilot"—and so three weeks before the pilot I called everybody I knew and said, "You know how to make TV?"

(Jim Sharp) I knew Ross from college. I didn't know him in college until graduation. We both went to the University of Puget Sound, and you know how at graduation you all get in a line in alphabetical order? Well it was Shafer, Sharp and we were in line for about an hour and it was 90 degrees that day and we started talking and we got to know each other in line. After that I started playing six feet and under basketball and the team I was on was looking for some players as close to six feet as possible and so I asked Ross if he wanted to come play with us and we got to know each other some more. At the time I loved writing and comedy, I grew up watching Carson every night and taped every Letterman show and when Ross got into stand up we were still friends and I started writing jokes for him.

Ross was just emerging as a legitimate, credible stand up. He'd won the Seattle Laugh Off, he was emerging on the national scene as a stand up, he was headlining around the county so he had kind of arrived and the Program Director came to Ross and said, "I don't know what the show is but I think it would be really cool if we had this comedy show that held court on local stuff"—and Ross came to me and said, "Hey, do you want to help me with this?"

(Dana Dwinell) Bob Jones asked me if I'd be interested in producing the show, and I said absolutely. It was difficult, I have to say, because my background was in talk and I'd done a lot of live specials.

(Jim McKenna) I think it was Monday and we've got this guy on who's won the Seattle comedy competition, his name is Ross Shafer, and he's there with his posse, a guy named Jim Sharp, a guy named Mike Neun, and I remember Dana [Dwinell] and I looking at each other and going, "Well this is the guy. I mean this guy is so obvious; he's the host that they're looking for."

(Bill Stainton) I have never met anyone as goal focused and achieves stuff like Ross does. He's kind of amazing that way.

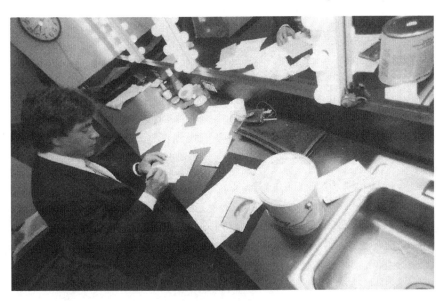

(Jim McKenna) If I remember right they gave Dana $1500 bucks (for production), they said that was all they had left in the line item. So Dana goes to her brother—there's so little faith in the show that she goes to her brother, her family was in the sign business— and asks her brother if he'll make her a neon sign that says Almost Live! But he doesn't have any faith in the show either and won't do it for her.

(Dana Dwinell) The neon was waaaay too costly. Somehow we bumped into the idea of bright colored plastic tubing that was lit by a black light to appear neon. Jim was right, though, that the ridiculous un-budgets imposed by KING Production and Program managers were the biggest and more contentious issues between all involved.

(Steve Wilson) Ross came out and does a monologue on the set of the then Seattle Today show, which we basically stripped of all furniture and filled with crap that was from my house—slot machine, telephone pole, all these props—hung them on the wall and said, "That looks goofy enough."

(Ross Shafer) We shot a pilot called Take 5 and they aired it and it wasn't awful, so the fall came around and they said, "We are going to go ahead and make 13 of these episodes. What do you want to call them?" So we got together, this little small team, it was Jim Sharpe who was the junior high school teacher who came up with the name Almost Live!.

(Bill Stainton) The show went on the air Sept. 23rd, 1984.

(Feliks Banel) When the show first started it was no big deal because there were so many minutes of local programming. Just KING alone had Seattle Today, Seattle Tonight, Pleasant Journeys. They had a fairly robust schedule of local programming.

(Tony Ventrella) I secretly admired the fact that somebody had the guts to put a local comedy show on the air. I was a huge supporter of the idea. You know, if it was up to me I would have put three comedy shows on our station.

(Jim Sharp) Ross would do a traditional monologue, he'd come out and hit his mark and tell his jokes. Most of them were local jokes, not all of them, and then we'd prepare an interview, we might have someone like Dave Niehaus on or somebody big in Seattle. If a celebrity was coming through town we'd try to grab them, and then for any given show we'd have four or even five sketches.

(Mike Neun) My role was to do comedy pieces that I wrote with Jim Sharp and Ross. I think I was the worst teleprompter reader in the history of television.

(Ross Shafer) We were lucky enough they didn't have anything else to put on the air. That's the reason we went into season two because they didn't have anything else, and the reason we had that time slot was that Al Wallace, the host of How Come?, died and they had to fill that half hour.

(Steve Wilson) We were on at 6pm on Sunday, which is considered the ghetto of local broadcasting. We were up against Town Meeting, which was Ken Schram, un-F-ing-beatable. Everyone would watch Ken Schram and then flip over to 60 Minutes. That's the way it worked.

(Bill Stainton) Ken Schram used to always beat us; we were opposite Town Meeting. For those first five years I don't know that we ever beat them in the ratings. I always wanted to get Schram on our show and he'd be like, "Yea, I'm trying to talk to the suits," because he wanted to come on, but it didn't happen.

(Jim McKenna) So we're on for an hour on Sunday nights, and it wasn't great. It was not a great show.

(Bill Stainton) I don't think the show was great at first. It's kind of like SNL where people think the original was so good, but if you actually watch the first season, they kind of sucked. The one nice thing we had was that, back then, we really only had three stations basically; cable wasn't a big deal. It was KING, KOMO and KIRO. So no matter how bad we were somebody was gonna watch us. And KING had this real devotion to local programming and it was a low budget show so it didn't really cost them much. So we could basically afford to suck for the first few years.

(Ross Shafer) We were allowed to fail, basically, and then come back next week and try to figure it out. It was not bad for us on the show, you know, in the beginning before it even aired the Seattle Times called us "Almost Dead".

(Mike Neun) Ross had been a football player in college and I realized that he was far better at shaking off bad nights than I was. We both worked as solo acts in comedy clubs, etc. and all comedians have nights that bomb. I think he viewed it as a bad game, shake it off and move on. I would be devastated and lose a lot of sleep.

(Jim Sharp) It wasn't very good but they didn't cancel us so we started learning how to do things. We had to do everything in those days, we'd sweep out the studio, warm up the audience, we were out on the streets of Seattle shooting stuff, and still, they didn't cancel us.

(Ross Shafer) The first season was such a "do it in your garage" production.

(Bill Stainton) We had our moments, we had some really, really good moments. I mean there were some sketches that were some of the best sketches the show ever did.

(Dana Dwinell) We'd bring in the studio audience; make sure everybody drank wine. That first year we won a bunch of local Emmys and we also won an Iris Award, which is a national award for excellence in local television. It was awesome.

(Jim McKenna) One thing I remember is that Dana didn't get a lot of respect from the cast. Her style of humor was not mine, but one of the things I learned quickly is that there are plenty of different comedy perspectives. She was a woman in a man's world at the time and never really got the credit she deserved in defending the show from those who wanted it cancelled. And that threat was very real. Dorothy Bullitt wasn't a fan. Sturges Dorrance, the Station Manager wanted it dead because he considered it a liability that would piss-off clients. Both Dana and I spent many hours defending the show to KING President Ancil Payne. We both knew he was a supporter and worked that angle to keep the show on the air for those first years, Dana way more than me.

(Ross Shafer) Dana Dwinell, who kind of took the job on a leap of faith, she was thrown to the wolves basically and did the best she could to coral this group of comedians who were trying to make TV. I don't think we were especially warm to her ideas but we had to do it because we didn't know anything; we didn't know what we were doing.

The Almost Live! Band. Michael Eads, Ricky Lynn Johnson, Steve Allen and Nick Moore.

Almost Live

Abbott and Costello. Martin and Lewis. Comedy yin and yang. You have the straight man and the funny guy. Ross was a funny guy but he was cut from straight man cloth. The one word that keeps coming up when describing Ross Shafer is smooth. The man had it in spades. He didn't look like a funny guy. He was handsome, too handsome for traditional funny guys, but he pulled it off. You don't win international comedy competitions with your looks. Keister on the other hand looked like a funny guy. He had a funny guy last name. Shafer and Keister had different styles that accommodated a wide spectrum of funny. It's like in baseball, if you've got one guy who hits lefties well and another guy who wears our right-handed pitching you've got a great one-two punch. No holes. That's how it was with Ross and John. But of course, when you've got two differing personalities and styles you can't expect smooth sailing the moment you cast off. However, professional respect and success have a way of calming the waters.

(John Keister) Before Almost Live! I was one of the editors at the Rocket magazine and a call came in, a random phone call came in and KING was starting the show REV (Rock Entertainment Videos) and they were looking for someone who could come over and talk about the local music scene, like a music news segment. It was before MTV had come to Seattle and whatnot, but there were lots of music videos circulating around and people were very interested in them and they found a way to package an hour's worth of them and I did what was called the Rocket Report. So I started joking a bit in the Rocket Report, it was the first time I had been on television and they said, "Hey, we are starting this other show up."

(Jim Sharp) When they told us they wanted John to join us I think we were a little suspicious about it because we didn't know him and it felt like he was being forced on us.

(Ross Shafer) Well, he came and they had some deal with him I think for a show called REV, and we said, "Okay, John, we will use you, you come up with something, show us what you have, show us your script and we will see what you do," because we didn't know him and I don't think he was very warm to us either. I don't think that he thought we very hip, frankly and that's fair, I was a guy who wore suit coats, here is a junior high school teacher (Jim Sharp), here is another comedian Mike Neun who was involved and Mike was an iconoclast, he didn't even want to be on television.

(Dana Dwinell) When John Keister came on board it was a little rough. His humor was quite different and Ross was not thrilled about it.

(Mike Neun) John was eager to take chances. We were different. I was trying to do Zen comedy, which I achieved about three times in 45 years, and he was more SNL. He was a hard worker, funny and really bright.

(John Keister) Ross and I had known each other from the comedy club days but it wasn't like we were friends exactly, we weren't enemies, we just didn't know each other very well and he was kind of like, he was sort of reticent, he didn't really know what I was about.

(Ross Shafer) Yeah, that was kind of arrogant of us, and the reason we had that skeptical attitude about John was that myself, Mike Neun, and Jim Sharp at that point, had really looked at comedy as some kind of science. The reason that I won that competition was because I had gone to a coach in San Francisco who taught me how to edit my act, he taught me how to count how many laughs I get per minute. It was clear to me that there were certain comedians that got on television and certain comedians that did not and the ones that got on television, because I had recorded them with my Sanyo VHS recorder, I would see what the comedians were doing in 6 minutes that I was not doing and it was because they were tightly edited, they would get six laughs a minute and each laugh would last for 3 seconds and they built it toward the end, and that penetrated the television screen. A lot of comedians that I would see who would work the comedy competition would ramble on and on, including myself, and eventually we might find a punch a line but that's not how the pros did it, and I wanted to do it like a pro and so did Jim Sharp. Mike Neun was a seasoned comedian; he had that already figured out.

(Mike Neun) I remember Jim Sharp being truly realistic about lines, grading them. "I think that's a 'C'," he'd say, and Ross would either agree or not but it was no big deal. It was the first time I'd seen that.

(Ross Shafer) So here is John Keister, a guy who was interested in music, how do you play into the mix? How he played into it was that he was just quirky. So the first meeting, and I will cut to the chase, after the first meeting we had with John two weeks went by and he didn't have anything. So, we thought, well maybe he is not taking us very seriously and maybe he will just go away, so then we put him on the spot and he said, "Okay, all right, I have this idea," nothing was written down, "I have this idea and I probably have the idea wrong and here is what sticks in my mind," and the idea was making fun of the Guardian Angels, they were very popular as a volunteer group, they were all the rage, and they scout for crime. But it's going to be called Guardian Anglers, these are guys who ride around their truck and they fish for crime, so I thought that was cool. No one ever thought like that. I said, "Do you have a script?" He said, "No, I am just going to go out and shoot it." Okay, all right. Somehow Dana arranged for us to get a camera and he went and shot this thing and came back and edited with a friend of his and we go, "Oh! Okay, now we get what you do," and we never asked for a script ever. And sometimes he would come into the meetings with these things written on cocktail napkins or toilet paper or a scrap of an envelope from a utility bill and we thought, this guy did it once, he could probably do it again.

(John Keister) I could see that Ross really enjoyed being the kind of attractive, well dressed successful guy and I am not like that and I thought there could be a lot of value in us playing that up.

(Dana Dwinell) There was a real different vibe between the two of them. Ross was a very smooth, Johnny Carson, Letterman-type host. He had a lot of stand up experience; he was glib.

(John Keister) I was sort of like the put-upon loser and he was the successful guy and it created this dynamic on the show that in the beginning worked really well, that people actually thought that he was always making fun of me, and people would stop me on the street saying, "You are the best, don't let him get you down."

(Dana Dwinell) What we clearly learned early on was that [John's] video pieces were the gems.

(Jim McKenna) I personally thought the best part was John's bits, the Assignment Danger segment. John was sort of the Chris Elliott character; his stuff was hysterical, he was a natural at writing. We would save his stuff for the end of the show because John's stuff was consistently 'A' material and we would try to hold the audience's attention 'til the end.

(Darrell Suto) Keister rose to fame there. It was his bits. Assignment Danger. That kind of stuff just started gathering. Remember that scene in Terminator 2 when that guy turns into liquid metal and you see the little drops pulling together? That's kind of what the show did.

(Jim Sharp) I remember the first piece John did, he was at one of the parks and he ate dirt and it was just fantastic, his first piece. It really worked and everybody loved it and it kind of took off from there.

(Pat Cashman) One of first things I think I ever did with John was an Assignment Danger sketch, which really was a great idea; it was his idea. He wanted to go and see the inside of Broadmoor, the neighborhood that's really rich and has these walls and – what it's like in there must be fantastic! These are rich people. So you see a scene of him putting up a ladder, climbing up the wall of Broadmoor and then when he jumps down on the other side we see he's in the most rural backwater part of South King County that we could find. We had to find the perfect place to shoot so we we're driving around and we said, "Goddamn, we've got to find the right place, it's got to be exactly the right place." I don't know where the hell we were but then we see this farmhouse and we are like, oh boy, this has got to be it. There was a bunch of sheep back there, walking around, and a rusty plough and weeds but it looked great. So I knock on the door and nobody is there. So we all look at each other and go, let's shoot here anyway. So it's somebody's private property and we're just, we go into the backyard and shoot.

(Mike Boydstun) I think John may have been basically working for free, I think he only got paid if his bits aired, and he only got paid a piddly amount, like $100 if they aired. John was kind of the renegade on the show. Ross Shafer and the head writer Jim Sharp were a little bit more conservative types and we were a little bit edgier. John would come up with a bit, I would shoot it and Ross would have the power to veto it if he chose to, but I don't remember him ever not running one of our bits.

(Ross Shafer) I don't think we ever didn't use one of his bits. Here is why, television is such a voracious animal for material content, we had never enough, and so if he came up with anything on video we put it on.

(John Keister) I think a real breakthrough was Ballard Vice. Ross really enjoyed playing the Ballard Vice guy, and it was interesting that other people around the area, like celebrity athletes and whatnot, liked those segments too and wanted to be, not just on the show, they wanted to be in that segment, that one in particular, Ballard Vice. It might be hard for you to remember but Miami Vice was a real trendsetter at the time and everybody dressed up and they were like the coolest guys and these athletes liked to come on.

(Jim Zorn) If you were to list the top five skits that they did, definitely the skit that I did with Chip Hanauer and my teammate Michael Jackson would be on there. We did a skit called Ballard Vice. The whole premise of the skit was Miami Vice, obviously, and we drove around and Chip Hanauer was smuggling halibut in the pontoons of his hydroplane and we were there to bust him.

(Mike Boydstun) Long before 9/11 we were shooting this bit called Ballard Vice with the Seahawk players Jim Zorn and Michael Jackson. I would shoot long lens so I'd be across the street from the action to make it look more cinematic, so I'd be shooting way across, I think I may have been on the fifth floor and they're running around with fake machine guns and there really wasn't any crew close to them so I'm surprised that we never raised any false alarms like people calling police. Because a scene like that where they're running around with machine guns in their hands—of course they're plastic from Toys R Us—but a big guy running around with no cameras close to him it's a pretty intimidating image. So I'm always amazed, particularly with that one that we managed to not scare the hell out of anybody.

(Ross Shafer) We were given such carte blanche to do anything we wanted, we never got a single permit. We charged onto property, we marched into Nordstrom, I had my shirt off and I had painted the numbers 44 on my bare chest and asked, "Where is your Brian Bosworth department?" Nobody said a word; nobody threw us out. I was kind of hoping that I might get thrown in jail because that would have made a great bit on the show.

(John Keister) Ross actually owned a Ferrari because he had a real good gig in this game show in Canada, so he had a Porsche and then a Ferrari; it was the mid '80s.

(Jim Sharp) Ross got some money, he was doing the radio show on KJR, he was doing Almost Live!, and I think the game show and he showed up one day in a red Ferrari. That was Ross being Ross.

(Ross Shafer) Yeah, I bought that with my radio money, radio paid you a lot more than television; radio was year around, television was only 13 weeks. I didn't have enough money from TV for that. What I can tell you is that everybody didn't share my joy or enthusiasm for that car except Keister, and Keister said this would be a lot better for Ballard Vice if we have this car.

(Joe Guppy) I was in that Ferrari once. It's cramped in there, I'll tell you. Not much more room than for your wallet and your butt.

(Mike Neun) He got five speeding tickets in about a month. He had to sell it before he went to jail, so he bought a Cadillac. When he gave Jay Leno a ride, Leno said, "Gee, what does your dad drive?"

A bird's-eye view of the split set.

Almost Live

1985

- VH1 debuts.
- Symbolics.com is the first .com domain name.
- The Titanic is located.
- The 76-story Columbia Center (Bank of America Tower) is completed. It becomes Seattle's tallest building.

1986

- Chernobyl disaster.
- Space Shuttle Challenger explodes after launch.
- Smoking banned on all public transports.
- Mike Tyson becomes the youngest heavyweight champion.

The Early Years

The first couple of years everyone was simply trying to get their feet under them while the show searched for its identity. These years introduced the first wave of performers to the show, outside of Ross and John. This was also the time that it became readily apparent that working on Almost Live! would be a job of passion, not profit.

(Jim Sharp) It wasn't a full time job. I had a little advertising agency that made really bad commercials for car dealers and carpet guys. Writing for Almost Live! was for fun and also comedy in television was kind of a dream so it was really, really great and cool and after a couple of years it actually started to work and people started watching the show.

(Bill Nye) It was a full time job for three weeks at a time. Every other month, I felt I had to scare up other work. I was probably wrong about the need to hustle constantly: "If I'm awake, I should be working." I worked as a freelance or "contract" engineer. I was one of the last guys, perhaps, who was comfortable working on a large drawing board with pencils (which we call "lead holders," and an "electric eraser," no kidding). I would get work designing specialty tooling or a part or assembly to fill small niches in the worlds of aerospace and instruments. I guess it led somewhere after all.

(Mike Boydstun) It was definitely a lot of work and we didn't have any support. I remember when I was doing the show we did a whole lot every week because at that time we had to fill an hour. I remember going out and shooting a Speed Walker with Bill Nye where the bit was somebody was taking a bolt out of the base of the Space Needle to make it fall and so we're shooting around the Seattle Center and I've got the camera on the tripod and I've got the boom mic wedged into my belt loop, so I'm running the camera and holding the boom because we didn't have wireless mics back then, just a shotgun microphone on a pole. I just remember having to do two jobs, three jobs at once because I had to do lighting too, so yea, it was a lot of work.

(Ross Shafer) We would borrow everything, we had to borrow cameras from the news division and they hated that, the news division hated it. When we had a meeting we had to see which conference room was not being used, when we started the only office we had was Dana's desk. I certainly had no desk, Jim Sharp had no desk, nobody had any place to really sit and then we would wander around the building asking KING employees if they would be extras.

(Mike Neun) Working the show was a great deal of fun, I admired the people I worked with and it was a learning experience. I don't think the money was very good, but hey, it was a local show with a lot of people on it. I have fond memories. While I worked on the show I also did concerts and shows elsewhere.

(Pat Cashman) I didn't even get paid for most of my time there until the last three or four years, which was fine with me because I had a full-time job. Even while I was getting paid it was pretty modest, I couldn't see how other people on the show were getting by on that, to tell you the truth.

(John Keister) I argued that we ought to have some other people on the show that could help out. I needed to work on the sketches and Ross really didn't have a lot of time to. If you can do sketches you have to direct them and you have to be pretty heavily involved in the editing process. It takes a lot of time. He really wasn't into that part of the business, he was from the part where you go on stage, you do your set and then you are done. He wasn't really comfortable hanging out for hours in an editing bay, just tweaking his stuff, but I was, in fact I really enjoyed it and so that's how the segments got made. There was a sketch group called the Off The Wall Players that Joe Guppy was in. We hired him. There were a couple of other people that we hired that came in kind of for a short term, one was Lynn McManus; she was a local actress in commercials. There was also Andy Stein; she was also in the Off The Wall Players.

(Andy Stein) I was on for the first two seasons as "the woman" with a bunch of young white guys. I had been a founding member of the Off The Wall Players, which was a comedy improv group. This started around 1980 at Bumbershoot so we were well-known and did a lot of shows and we did a little short bit for REV, the show that John was on, so that's how we became familiar with John and John became familiar with us. Joe Guppy was one of the members of Off The Wall Players and he was part of the original cast of Almost Live! so when they needed a woman to come on board I was recommended. We were all writer/performers. I was on for two seasons before I moved to LA because I thought I wanted to continue working as an actress. I was very fortunate in that the show allowed me to create a nice demo reel so I was able to take that down with me and I was able to get representation. My first show was the Bob Newhart show. I was also on Murphy Brown, Lois and Clark, a Stevens Segal movie called Hard to Kill.

(Joe Guppy) I came on in '85. Keister recruited me for the show. He knew my work from REV. For REV, which was originally hosted by Roger Fisher of Heart, we took these music videos and hosted it  from a local club and it would have local bands as well. But we needed comedy, so they put in pieces from my comedy group called Off The Wall Players. And also there was the Rocket Report with John Keister, and I believe that was the first television for Keister. So when he got on Almost Live! he has lunch with me and asks me if I'd like to get in on this show thing. I said okay.

(Nancy Guppy) John cherry-picked Joe, not only because he was funny but because he felt he had the ambition and ability to do TV. He had the structure and discipline. He was on about a year and Joe would use me on  occasion because we were dating and he would say, "Hey, can you get off work?" I worked at Nordstrom in the credit department.

He'd say, "We need you to play a girlfriend of Ross in a bit." Then I'd lie and say I had a doctor's appointment, get off work and go do the thing. So there was a year of that; then I got a chance to write some sketches. They were not very good, but they were good enough that the producer, Bill Stainton decided to hire me.

(Bill Nye) Ross Shafer approached me at Swannie's Comedy Underground after a set I did on a Monday open mic night. Not sure what he was thinking. Once I got hired, a big distraction for me was the small pay and the part time schedule. I had an engineering job. I was a professional with a mortgage and able to get credit at The Bon Marche! Leaving that lifestyle and salary, as well as losing the intellectual challenge of mechanical design was always on my mind. If I stayed out of engineering too long I'd never be able to get a good job again. Ross suggested I take a part-time job as a waiter.

(Pat Cashman) When they were putting Almost Live! on the air, it quickly exhausted their staff, because they had to do an hour every week. And it shows what a hungry animal TV is, so they started seeing if anybody else wanted to participate in this show. So I did.

(John Keister) At that time Pat was doing these really humorous promos for KING. He had such a mastery of timing and editing that we learned a lot from him.

(Pat Cashman) I was the Creative Director with nobody under me at all. It was a great job. I got to do these promos for the news, for all the different shows, and more often than not they let me to make funny ones, which is kind of unusual for news promo.

(Scott Schaefer) After graduating from Eastern Washington University I came back from Cheney to Seattle and thought that I would just get a job in television right away and I found that that's not how it worked in the real world. I'd known of Almost Live!, it had just finished its first season and I thought I could work on this show so I submitted some scripts for sketches. This would have been in the summer of 1985 and John Keister, who was second banana at the time, was the taped bit guy on the show. I submitted tens sketches with a friend of mine and they bought one of them and I remember distinctly how excited I was. It was a sketch called Assignment Danger where Keister found this remote control that controlled real life very much like the Adam Sandler movie Click, only many years earlier. I asked if I could help out on the shoot for the sketch and they said sure and we really hit it off. Afterwards I basically said if you need any more help on any shoots I'm willing to work for free. They called me the next week and bought a couple more scripts. It was about three months before they hired me as a part time writer. It was the same week that they hired Joe Guppy and Bill Nye, and I believe we were all paid the same which was about $130 a week. They said we can only pay you a part-time salary but pretty much everybody came down every day to work while holding down some other job. In the evenings I was selling over the phone Fishing and Hunting News to make my rent. I was working 12 hour days, I was young, I was excited about working in television; the next year I got promoted to associate producer and I think my salary went up to $460 a week and I was able to quit my Fishing and Hunting News job.

(Andy Stein) I was thinking, I can't believe I'm being paid for this, this is terrific! The days would go where you would sit down at the big table, you would pitch ideas and if one of your ideas was chosen you grabbed the camera crew and go and shoot on location. It was very exciting to go out with a camera crew and have an idea that you thought about come to life.

(Joe Guppy) I was thinking, I can't believe I'm barely getting paid for this. But it finally became decent money. Well, decent money for a Seattle artist. It was a really super fun job.

(Scott Schaefer) During the seasons that I was on the show somebody would do something funny or interesting and we'd all say, "Oh that'll be in the book." But nobody ever wrote a book about Almost Live! (authors note: Ha!). We would do these pranks like I would write up a script and I'd want to make it look as official as possible and give it to Ross in the writers meeting and say, "Here Ross, read the script," and he would read it cold and of course we would just fill it with obscenities because we just wanted to hear Ross say all these bad words. He'd pick up the script and read, "So have I ever told you how much I like to (insert F-bomb)?" We didn't think he'd actually say it because Ross never dropped the F-bomb. It actually worked about three times. He stopped reading them cold after that.

(Ross Shafer) Yes, yes, I remember that, I do remember that. I didn't swear much around Scott Schaefer because he was so young.

(Mike Boydstun) On one level it was the greatest local TV gig you could have. On another level it was a whole lot of work and we all wanted it to be really good so it got frustrating. That's why I eventually left because after a while you just want to do higher quality. It wears on you after a bit. But for the most part it was the best job you could have.

(Bill Nye) I felt great about my work. But the rate of pay, and the need to continually supplement my income with freelance engineering contract work was always on my mind. I was continually wondering how long I could stay in television.

(Mike Neun) Being the supreme judge of talent that I am, I think I totally overlooked the skills of Jim Sharp and Bill Nye. Of course, they were the two who went on to truly big things. Then again, I saw Bob Dylan at the Monterey Folk Festival and knew at once he was no big deal.

(Dana Dwinell) Early in the second season Bob Jones left the station to go to Philadelphia and hired me to do a morning show out there. I was in the midst of trying to renegotiate with Keister, the band, Jim, Ross, and KING was still not coming through with the money, despite the successes we'd had. They weren't giving any money, everybody was really pissed and everybody was mad at me because there was no money so when Bob says, "Do you want to come to Philadelphia?" I said, "That's not a bad idea."

(Bill Stainton) I came in half way through the second season to replace Dana Dwinell. Dorothy Bullitt, and this is what was so cool about KING, Dorothy was really committed to local programming. I remember she told me once, "We are absolutely here to serve the public." We don't hear that much these days in TV. She said, "Don't get me wrong, we're going to make a profit while we're doing it; we're not a charity." So she wanted to serve the public in as many ways as possible. KING had a really healthy documentary unit, our news was great, and so this was a way to look at things through a different lens, the lens of comedy. Turns out she was never really a fan of the show but she liked having it on.

(Joe Guppy) I don't think it was a bad show. Any ranking comedian who was coming through town would be on the show. Dana Carvey was on the show, Jerry Seinfeld was on the show, Ellen DeGeneres was on the show.

(Ross Shafer) We had quite a few memorable guests. There was Joe Walsh from the Eagles.

(Bill Stainton) I remember calling him, because he was in his limo. KISW was bringing him into town. So I said, "Okay, Joe, so here's the thing, we have a band, would you be willing?" And he says, "Yea, have them learn Rocky Mountain Way in G." This is a couple of days before the show. So they learned it, and I remember being in the studio when they rehearsed, there were six people in the studio when they rehearsed, four guys in the band, Joe Walsh and me. I'm thinking, I'm Lorne Michaels, this is so freaking cool.

(Ross Shafer) So Joe came in and his first request was, "Where is the dressing room?" We showed him the dressing room, and he said, "Now I need a quart of Vodka."

(Steve Wilson) Joe Walsh had a rider on his contract and that rider was a fifth of vodka and it had to be in the freezer. And he consumed that entire fifth of vodka before he went on.

(Ross Shafer) It was gone before he got on the show.

(Steve Wilson) He played Rocky Mountain Way with the band and then came over and did an interview with Ross! He did two segments. I mean, it's F-ing Joe Walsh! You kidding me? I didn't care what condition he was in.

(Bill Stainton) Joe Walsh should have been terrible, he drank a fifth of vodka before he went on the show but he was a phenomenal guest.

(Ross Shafer) He really delivered, he played with our band, played Rocky Mountain Way, which was at that time, this was beyond cool and then I asked him some questions and I said, "You are a writer but you travel with a chain saw, is that true?" He goes, "That's true, I do." I said, "Why do you travel with a chain saw?" And he said, "You know, when you check into hotels and they tell you you have a connecting room but it's not..." It would just blew people away that we could have that kind of performance on this little television show.

(Bill Stainton) Let's see, what other guests. Joe Namath was really cool, Tiny Tim was an amazing person, very, very strange but one of the two most polite people I've ever met in my life, the other being Harry Connick Jr. Ellen DeGeneres stands out. We were her second TV show ever, the first being Johnny Carson. I remember watching Carson and the next day calling her people and asking if she could be in Seattle on Saturday. She's completely delightful; I was a huge Ellen fan from that moment on.

(Ross Shafer) Jerry Seinfeld was our guest, and we knew that it was pretty cool to have him, he had done the Tonight Show a lot; we got a reputation where we could get anybody coming to Seattle to do our show.

(Bill Stainton) Seinfeld was the first comedian I ever booked for the show. When he came I asked him to do five minutes of stand up and he said, "I don't do stand up anymore unless it's Carson or Letterman." I basically said, "C'mon Jerry, this is my first full season doing this and everybody's looking at me, can you just do it this one time?" – and he did me a favor and said, "Okay, all right, I'll do it." And he did it and came up with these customized Seattle jokes. He did me a big favor then. He broke his own rule.

(Ross Shafer) We had Phil Donohue on. He had a new talk show and he thought that he was going to dominate, then Oprah just blew him away and I asked him if his hair had gone white before or after Oprah. He took it seriously. He said it actually started in high school and he didn't know what to do about it. I don't think he realized there was supposed to be a joke in there somewhere.

(Bill Stainton) Phil Donohue was a son of a bitch. I despised him; he was terrible. Miserable interview, he made us jump through hoops to get him on the show.

(John Keister) The guest who had the most impact for me was my friend Kenny G; we were in the same class in high school. He was super popular at that time and still is, and the show was not going well and I just called him up and I said, "Kenny, I need some help, would you be on the show?" and he was like, "Yeah, sure, what do you need me to do?" and I said, "I need you to promote that you are going to be on the show," and so we took him down to Pike Place Market and he like, was busking, and people were coming by and going, "Man, you really have Kenny G down!"

Almost Live

Bill Nye the Science Guy

Almost Live! had its share of success stories and Bill Nye is certainly near the top of that list. But what makes Bill's success so fascinating is that you couldn't have picked a more unlikely candidate. He was a Boeing engineer, for crying out loud. Hardly a hotbed for developing nation-wide celebrity. But he had one thing in his favor: a uniquely different perspective.

(John Keister) I knew Bill from the comedy clubs in the early '80s. He was a Boeing engineer who did stand up comedy. He was also a Big Brother and he also volunteered in children's educational things, so if you look at what the Bill Nye the Science Guy show is it involves all of what Bill did, he was really into children's education, he is a scientist and he was a comedian, and if you look at the show, it was synthesis, that's Bill, it's not a character really.

(Ross Shafer) Bill Nye and I got to know each other as we are both competing in the comedy competition and we would ride together and we would hang out together and he had a good job, he had a job at Boeing and Nordstrom I think, making wing parts for airplanes and he was also a stand-up comedian. He could be hilarious some night and other nights he bombed. He was still quirky, still an odd character and I just loved him, and so we brought him on the show as a writer and I think he was getting $75 a week or maybe $50, anyways it was a pain for him to get there because he would ride his bicycle or motorcycle to get to the meetings.

(Scott Schaefer) He really is a science guy and he would come up with some really strange ideas at our meetings, and we would think, Man, this guy is really strange, he's got a different sense of humor.

(Bill Stainton) Bill Nye was the guy who would come up with a hundred ideas. Ninety-nine would be complete crap, but that hundredth one was something no one else could come up with.

(John Keister) Bill wasn't really a writer, Bill didn't write a lot of sketches, but he really had a very, very strong presence and was very useful on the show.

(Ross Shafer) He tried a few bits that we liked, he was a character player, Speed Walker I think was one of his bits, and he was in some of the Billy Quan stuff, but anyway, the story that I like to tell and still tell is that one week we lost a guest on short notice...

(Bill Nye) My recollection is that Rita Jenrette cancelled her visit to Seattle. When Ross Shafer performs on stage and talks about this, he says it was Geraldo Rivera. He may be absolutely right, but I believe it was Ms. Jenrette, and I certainly understand why Ross uses Mr. Rivera to tell the same story. Geraldo is still famous; no 'splainin' is necessary. Ms. Jenrette was notorious for having had sex on the steps of the US Capitol building. And get this: the guy she was having sex with was her husband... of all people. I mean that's just weird. Married people don't have sex with each other, do they?

(Ross Shafer) We had to put something on the air, we had a giant hole in the schedule now and Bill was sitting there, going through his magazine, and we asked Bill if he had any demonstrations or something that he could do in front of people that would be amazing. We could call him our science correspondent and I said, "We will just call him Bill Nye the Science Guy." Bill blurts out,

"I could do something pretty hilarious with a tub of liquid nitrogen," and I remember thinking, Who does things like that? And I asked, "Can you get liquid nitrogen?" "Yeah, I know a couple of people, I can get it. We have this spot over here, okay, let's try it." And it wasn't more planned than that. We didn't even ask him what he was going to do with this liquid nitrogen, we put him on and it was an instant hit.

(Bill Nye) I volunteered my time at the Pacific Science Center as a "Science Explainer"; I wore a blue vest, etc. I spent a lot of time with liquid nitrogen, which looks dangerous. But, nitrogen is most of what is between you and your computer screen. When it comes to breathing it, we animals have it down— completely non-toxic (at standard pressure). The way I remember it, Ross said roughly, "Bill, why don't you do that stuff you're always talking about; you could be Bill Nye the Science Guy, or something…" Then, he closed his fine leather briefcase and hustled out of the building to do his afternoon drive show on KJR, which was still an AM station back then, and still the main afternoon drive radiobroadcast. I'm pretty sure that as I discussed the hilarious comedy gags (?) that I did at the Science Center, Jim Sharp suggested I do the "Household Uses" of the stuff, of liquid nitrogen.

(John Keister) So Bill did this bit called "Cooking with Liquid Nitrogen" and lo and behold it became a real thing called molecular gastronomy. If you watch Top Chef or any of the high end cooking shows they make a big deal of it. And here was Bill, back in the day, doing it as a joke. Another creation unleashed into the world by Almost Live!

(Scott Schaefer) It was this great display that nobody had ever seen, he dipped whatever it was he had in the liquid nitrogen and the fog was billowing out all over the studio and then he smashed it on the ground and it shattered and it made a great visual. I think later Bill did two more segments like that and they were very popular, really unusual comedy because nobody was doing comedy science.

(Bill Nye) I messed around and found that onions and celery [in liquid nitrogen] were pretty compelling gags. Celery gets turgid or tumescent or stiff. Onions make the sound of broken glass. What's not to love? The payoff was, and is still the payoff for me with liquid nitrogen: Chew frozen marshmallows, and steam comes out of your nose. I admit that I had and have spent quite a bit of time chewing frozen marshmallows. There is a little bit of a trick to not burning your tongue and maximizing the steamy effect. I was in cross training for this bit. I was and still am a regular reader of Science News magazine. I carefully tossed in some stuff about theobromine being an aphrodisiac.

(Ross Shafer) I remember the lab coat, I think it was this smock that we got from the Ed Hume show, and I tell the audience, "We never have enough science in the show," and I looked at the producer, "Have we ever had science?" "No." "See, not at all." So here it is, Bill Nye the Science Guy, and then he does this series of demonstrations and it was just so good and it was something that we could never have seen coming. So afterwards I said, "That's amazing, Bill, we have to do it again," and I'll remember this till I die, he says, "Yeah, I am surprised that you guys hadn't already thought of that."

(Bill Nye) As soon as I walked toward the sideline or wing of the stage, I knew, I just knew I was on to something. Scott Schaefer said to me, almost under his breath, "There's your recurring character…" When you're a cast member on a show like Almost

Live!, or dare I claim, Saturday Night Live, what you want is a recurring character.

(Scott Schaefer) Not long after that he came with all of these pens and started handing them all out to everybody and they said Bill Nye the Science Guy on them and it didn't have a trademark mark on it it had an SM, a Service Mark on it, and he said he was going to trademark the phrase Bill Nye the Science Guy and we are all like, What?! How much is that going to cost? And I think it was something like $1500 and we thought he was crazy. What are you doing? And of course he was right all along.

(Bill Nye) I did indeed bring in some pens. They were "process blue," a standard royal blue kinda color. They feature a clear piece fitted in the barrel, so you could watch the mechanism as you clicked. I felt they were consistent with my vision for The Science Guy® and The Science Guy™ (I, as a brand, get the ® symbol; objects like t-shirts and pens get the ™ symbol; that's how our patent & trademark system rolls). I'm not sure my fellow writers laughed as such, but there was skepticism. I guess my colleagues didn't realize how much I really am into science and how profound was my frustration with US management practices that gave us the Ford Pinto, the Chevy Vega, and leisure suits. Along with the trademark filing I was already answering listener questions on Ross's radio show every afternoon at 4:35.

(Ross Shafer) I had him on every day because what I found out about Bill is that you could ask him anything and he would come up with either the real response or a very convincing BS response. People call my radio show, "Yeah, hi Bill, how come I sneeze when I look at the Sun?" And then Bill would talk for a minute about why the filtration of Sun rays and this and that and even if you didn't know it was untrue you thought, Well, he said it, he is a

Science Guy; he knows enough. You can ask him things about dinosaur, space, or bacteria, there is no limit; this guy had been this Science Guy his whole life.

(Bill Nye) Every morning at 6:00 am, I watched, and re-watched Don Herbert's "Mr. Wizard's World." When I was a kid, his show was black & white, and it was called "Watch Mr. Wizard." Years later, I met Don Herbert and his wife Fern. She told me that Don was very pleased that he had passed the torch to me. Sometime after that, just as Don had, I received the Science Advocacy Award from the Council for Elementary Science International (part of the National Science Teachers Association, NSTA). I get choked up just [talking] about it. I messed around with Don's demonstrations quite a bit. I very much wanted to influence the future, young people. So, I quit my day job October 3rd, 1986. Before January of 1987 was out, I came up with the Science Guy on television.

Louie Louie

In 1985 Almost Live! led a charge to change our state song from Washington, My Home to Louie Louie: the 1963 hit song by the Kingsmen, whose mostly-indecipherable lyrics were laughingly investigated by the FBI for two years because they thought they might be obscene. Surprisingly, the state song push made news for 210 straight days and a whole lot of people took notice. Close to 5000 supporters rallied on the steps of the state capitol and World News Tonight was there. Esquire magazine awarded them the coveted Dubious Achievement award. The Whatcom County Council even passed Resolution No. 85-12 asking the state legislature to make Louie Louie the state song, and to name a newly created county Louie Louie County. When it came to a final vote in the Washington State House, however, the politicians said nope. For what it's worth Louie Louie is recognized as the *unofficial* rock song of Washington State. It's also the 7th inning stretch song during Mariners games following Take me out to the Ball Game. So we've got that going for us.

(Dana Dwinell) The Louie Louie campaign was huge. I'm sure other people will take credit for it but I'm gonna say Jim Sharp and Jim McKenna had a lot to do with it. Somehow we were sitting in this room thinking we have to do something for this second season to break out and create some buzz. Jim or Ross I think said, "How about a state song?" Someone, I forget whom, suggested Louie Louie. So Jim Sharp knew a legislator and thought he could get him to introduce it on the senate floor. And it all just sort of happened. The point was never to get Louie Louie to be the state song, the point was to make a ruckus and get people to pay attention to Almost Live!. And the first thing that happened was that ABC News and People magazine picked up on it.

(Jim McKenna) I went with Ross to Olympia and we shot a sketch where he tries to get it introduced as a bill before the legislature. We also did a parody of the old "Show us your Lucky Strikes" campaign where we had people show us their Louie Louie button. That was really all there was to it, until some citizens picked up on it.

(Ross Shafer) Any time you have an idea like that you have no idea whether it's going to work, it's all completely up to your audience. If they buy into it then they are going to carry it and we would try to execute along the way. This idea had a life of its own.

We created a controversy because a woman who had written the original state song, Helen Davis, was still alive and she was 86. I don't remember the lyrics, some of the lines are *Washington, My home, wherever you may roam, fields of wheat*, I don't know what it was, silly song. I grew up in that era and I never heard that song in school. But she was torqued that these young guys on this TV show were going to unseat her song, so she went to the competing station in Spokane, and said, "If that Ross Shafer wants to change the state song to Louie Louie he might as well change the state flower to marijuana." It was explosive, it was kind of the ammunition that we could work with and I played her a little bit and then I went on TV and said, "Helen, we appreciate the song but look, one campaign at a time, we are so swamped right now with this, we can't possibly take anything else on."

(Jim Sharp) It was just a joke. It got more attention than I thought it would and the media and some politicians actually had some fun with it. It took on a life of its own for a while, but I never thought it would be adopted as the state song.

(Jim McKenna) We were shocked, but totally pumped about how well the idea worked. It went way beyond anybody's expectations.

Shooting the sketch of Ross pitching Louie Louie to the
Washington State Legislature

Ross became a regular on Dick Clark's Bloopers and Practical
Jokes to promote Louie Louie as our state song

Almost Live

1987

- FOX broadcasting debuts.
- The Simpsons debuts on the Tracey Ullman show.
- Stock market crashes—loses 508 points—22.6%—on Oct. 19[th.]
- England and France begin digging the Chunnel.

The Lure of LA

Los Angeles is TV's major leagues—the pinnacle of the business. For anybody with the requisite ambition going to LA is a no-brainer. It's the west coast's version of New York, New York: If you can make it there you can make it anywhere. Many of the Almost Live! cast and crew knew it and felt the draw. Going to LA is one thing, succeeding in LA is another, and staying there is a completely different animal. Once you've had a taste of the luxuries available it's difficult to give them up. Imagine being given the keys to a Lamborghini and then having to go back to your old Toyota. Of course, fast, expensive cars have their own issues and there's a lot to be said for the comfort and familiarity of your old car. Some Almost Live! players were content with their 4-door sedan, others were not.

(Jim McKenna) I left in '87. I'd been down in LA with my wife; I was considering practicing my craft down there. My wife was fabulously wealthy, an heiress from Mercer Island, and she decided we were going to buy a brand new Acura and have a romantic drive down the coast and move to LA, maybe because she had family down there. I remember once I got down there I thought, I can't do this, I can't raise my family in this place. So I decided to come back to Seattle and make TV that nobody sees for the rest of my life. All of a sudden Dana calls up and says I need to fly back up to Seattle and talk to management about taking over Almost Live! because she was leaving to go to Philadelphia. So I called the manager and said, "Let's talk about how to move the show on," and she goes, "Don't bother, don't bother coming in." And I'm like, "What?" But I finally got the meeting and when I sit down she says, "I never really got Almost Live!, I don't get the sensibility."

(John Keister) She not only didn't get the sensibility of Almost Live!, she hated it. She was from the national office of Evening Magazine and literally that was the only thing she knew how to do on television. She was a very tiny woman but she struck fear into everyone in the production department. People were terrified of her.

(Jim McKenna) And I'm kind of looking at her like, I can't believe this woman is saying this. She came from Evening Magazine out of San Francisco and she says she wants to make the show more like Evening Magazine, and I remember blurting out, "For God's sakes, don't make it like Evening Magazine," and I remember seeing in her face, zip, that's it, that was all I needed to hear to convince me not to hire you. So I fly back to LA and I tell my wife, "I don't think I'm going to get the gig." So when I'm driving back up the coast, I'm taking a tour of KGW-TV in Portland, KING's sister station, and my buddy Craig Smith worked there, and as he's giving me this tour and he shows me this game show set and says, "Yea, we lost our producer, he's going up to Seattle to produce this show called Almost Alive, or something like that." And I'm like, "Oh,"—and he can see in my face something was wrong. I still thought I had a shot at the job.

(Ross Shafer) The more we did that show the more ambitious I became about taking it to the next level. I was a kid who grew up loving Johnny Carson on the Tonight Show and it was maybe two years in when I thought, Oh my god, Carson is going to get old and they will start looking for replacements, maybe I could be a replacement? I knew Jay Leno from the comedy clubs and met Dave [Letterman] once and they were great, but I kind of had in my mind, that job is accessible, that there is way to get that job.

(Jim Sharp) I don't think [Ross] was looking to leave Almost Live!. As a comic and television personality it seems normal to want to perform at the highest level.

(Nancy Guppy) Everyone wanted to go national. That's what we would call it, "We're gonna go national!" That was the desire of everyone on that cast, certainly from those early days. No question about it.

(Ross Shafer) When I first started doing Almost Live! and I saw the potential in it, we were winning awards and I honestly went to KING TV [management] weekly and said, "If we can get this show seen by any of KING's sister stations—Portland, Spokane…" I think we have four others—I think maybe Boise too—and they said, no. I tried to explain that this is the kind of show that would play at other places. But they didn't take it seriously enough or think that it was something that they could re-market.

(Bill Stainton) [Ross] was very frustrated with KING's disinterest in putting the show on the other stations. I seem to recall a meeting where we pled the case that we could still keep the "localness" of the show ("local" would, in this case, mean Pacific NW rather than just Seattle) while expanding our appeal to Portland and Spokane. But…that never happened.

(Ross Shafer) I told them we didn't want more money, we just wanted people to see it and enjoy it, kind of build our brand so to speak and when they kept saying no, kept saying no, kept saying no, then I go into my agent saying, "Okay, they keep saying no, can you guys sell this show? Can we take Almost Live! into syndication or anything else?" And so, at that point, my agent was William Morris and they were pretty powerful, so they tried to sell the show and it got a lot of attention but they felt like it was just too local and William Morris said, "I think we could sell *you.*" And so, I said, "All right, let's see what happens, and if we are in the right situation then I can pitch Almost Live! as a network show and it's a way for KING TV to make money." How could they say no? And we actually asked, I think it was the USA Network that was interested and I said, "I think we have a buyer for Almost Live!," and they still said no. Now I was really frustrated and went back to the agent and said, "Do you think you can put me on a show? I would love to see what we can do."

In 1987 Joan Rivers began hosting the Late Show on the fledgling Fox network. It was this decision that infamously infuriated her mentor Johnny Carson; he felt betrayed. As a result he never spoke to her again. The show did not do well. Several rumors swirled about the cause of the show's demise: Middle-America siding with Carson, Joan's husband Edgar Rosenberg clashing with Fox executives—whatever the reason Joan was gone after a single year. Fox had a show with no host.

(Ross Shafer) Joan Rivers started her show in '87 and I remember watching Joan and thinking our show is just as good as that Late Show she does. This is unbelievable. How does she get away with that? How does she do that? If we had that opportunity, that would be amazing.

(John Keister) No one saw that Joan Rivers was going to flame out as fast as she did. It was kind of a shock because I thought she was going to be good competition to Johnny Carson but she really flamed out and then they started looking for a replacement host and they were trying a lot of people out, dozens really. Dennis Miller did a joke, once, he said, "I have been avoiding going to Los Angeles because I am afraid I might be asked to host the Late Show, seemed to be like jury duty."

(Ross Shafer) Fox network has this show and they are running guest hosts through nightly, and Arsenio Hall was one. He could be a great fit and he did it over and over but he had some other activities going and every time he was not there the ratings would suffer, so Fox offered him the permanent host job and he said no because at that point he realized that he had some heat in late night and his agent brought him in to host his own show in syndication. Now Fox still has no host.

(Jim Sharp) All the affiliates had a deal with Fox that they would keep the show on for two years, and Joan left after I think one year. They had to provide programming to fulfill their contract.

(Ross Shafer) So there were Bob Newhart and you pick the name, it could be anybody, there were lots of people who were trying after that job and my agent got me on that list.

(John Keister) I mean they tried a lot of big name comics through there but Ross, he hosted a show and there were a lot of bits and routines we had developed that he could use. Because of that he had kind of a leg up on a lot of those people.

(Jim Sharp) [Almost Live!] was winning awards and getting noticed and we kind of learned how to do some stuff right and Ross was a good host and he was a funny comedian. He crafted his jokes, they were well constructed, he was really good at set up/punch line, and he was a good-looking guy so he got the call.

(Ross Shafer) We taped [Almost Live] on Thursday nights so I went down there Friday and did the Friday night network show. They picked me up in a limousine and took me to the studio and I did some mock interviews in the afternoon and then did their show and did monologue jokes from Almost Live! on the show.

(Jim McKenna) I watched those first two nights that he was on the Late Show and he was on fire! Oh my F-ing God, the audience is just roaring and everything is an 'A' joke.

(Ross Shafer) So then after the show the network executives said,

"We want to offer you this job," and I said, "Okay, that's awesome," and I said, "I've got to finish the season in Seattle." Then they said, "Well, we can't have you finish the season, you've got to start Monday." Wow! Then I called my agent, I talked to KING and asked is there a way I could fly back into Seattle and do Almost Live! and then go to LA, because people do that, but it didn't work out. Bill Stainton was our producer at that point and he didn't see that was practical and so we taped Almost Live! on a different day and I really tried to be accommodating but I didn't want to let this big fish fall off the line, the Fox thing, and I also had a radio show at that time on KJR and that was even stickier because that was a daily afternoon drive show.

(John Keister) I don't think the stations saw that coming because if they had they would have signed him to a contract. They screwed up.

(Ross Shafer) If you look up "how to burn a bridge" that's my story.

(Mike Neun) I think Ross going to LA was a career move that made a lot of sense. His choice was to stay on a great local show in Seattle for the rest of his life, or move on to bigger and better things. He had a chance to do network television and become a big star. I'm sure we talked about it and I probably gave him some terrible advice because I'm really good at that.

(Pat Cashman) I'm sure Fox would have moved on quickly if he didn't snatch the chance. I would think anyone who would have been in a similar position would have done the same. After all, most people would think of a local show as a stepping-stone for something bigger.

(John Keister) Ross was allowed to go down and do the audition; they thought it was just going to be for one night and they were like, "Oh sure, you can do that," but I can tell you that Joe Guppy and I were pretty sure he wasn't coming back, just talking amongst ourselves.

(Ross Shafer) Yeah, the stations were not happy and they should have been unhappy. If I had been in their position I would have been unhappy too. Now here is the irony of that, the irony is my agent has been predictive in what might happen to me, so in our contracts it always said, if Ross did a national show he is able to move on that level and both KJR and KING signed up on that, so I was certainly within my legal rights to do it, just the timing was horrible.

(John Keister) Yeah, it hit them real hard. They had just lost Donohue and they were still reeling from that. Then they find out Ross is staying in California, which they couldn't prevent, because they didn't have a contract with him. This new regime were major screw ups.

(Bill Stainton) There was some friction there at first. Ross was put into sort of a bad situation. He got this offer that you can't refuse. It was his chance to be Johnny Carson. A late night talk show host on a network. And he got it! Unfortunately he didn't know quite how to handle it so the next call I got was from one of his agents saying Ross isn't coming back.

Ross was gone and Almost Live! had no host. Changing hosts on a successful TV show is an iffy proposition at best. Audiences form a bond with on-camera talent; they become familiar with their style, their patter, their rhythm. When a familiar face leaves it doesn't take long before viewers decide whether or not the interloper is worth inviting into their home. It's particularly scary for the TV show's cast and crew because TV execs have notoriously itchy trigger fingers. Ross Shafer left big shoes to fill and they needed to fill them, pronto.

(John Keister) Ross did his last show and then there was I think about five guys who guest-hosted.

(Tony Ventrella) After Ross left I immediately went to the producer and said, "I know I'm a sportscaster, I have a contract, I know that things are going well but I'd like to audition to host Almost Live!."

(John Keister) Tony Ventrella hosted one. I hosted one; we had this guy from PM magazine who hosted one.

(Pat Cashman) I guest-hosted it at one time.

(John Keister) I asked them [if I would be the permanent host] and they said, "Well, we can't commit to that." I said, "You mean you can't tell me right now that I am going to be the host of this show," and they were like, "No, we can't say that now," and so I was like, "What do you think I am going to be? Someone else's sidekick; that I am going to be the permanent [Almost Live!] sidekick?" So,

Ross had been at that time saying, "Why don't you come down and be on the Late Show and you can work here."

(Ross Shafer) What happened at the network level, and it was something that I didn't think would happen, I was naïve I suppose, I'd gotten the head job, they even put my name on the show and all that, and then they felt they had the wisdom to pick chemistry for my sidekick. So I would be introduced to these people I didn't know, one of them was David Spade. I didn't know David Spade but they thought that he would be a good sidekick for me but David didn't like me and I didn't have any chemistry with him and I think he was so young, whatever his age, but he looked so young, it looked like I was his dad. It just wasn't a good fit and so I said, "I got the guy, I know the guy who can do this, we worked together for five years, we know each other and we know how to push each other's buttons and it will be great." So I had John come down and we had the best show probably that we had ever got at Fox with John as this guy down the couch who makes smart remarks, bails out awkward moments and he looks completely different than I look. They offered him the job, so he was perfect, it was magic and Jim Sharp was there, Scott Shafer was there; we put the band back together, so to speak.

(John Keister) So I went down there a couple of weeks and suddenly I was on the air down there and Hollywood, it was exactly the way I thought it would be. All the big celebrities of the day were coming on the show as guests and so it was like the cast of LA Law and Playboy Bunnies and all this sort of stuff and it was going really well. The other thing is I met some people who would become very important in my writing career, the writers on the show who went on to be fairly major players in the industry and I got to be friends with them and I enjoyed that. But there were a couple of things going on, one was my wife at that time, we just found out that we were going to have twins right around this time and I kind of looked around LA and I could see this is a job that would be 24-hours-a-day. It was 24-hour-a-day job being in show business in Hollywood and it was a very, like, I could see that it was going to be difficult for me because it was kind of a place where they would give you anything, anything you wanted and, "Hey, we need a couple of Ferraris for this sketch." "What color?" and, "I want to drink before the show." "Oh, what do you want?" The fact that I was on air, suddenly I got my own dressing room, and I got this and that and I could see this was going to really be a difficult thing for me because I wasn't the most stable person on the planet and this was going to be real dangerous for me.

(Ross Shafer) It was intoxicating, the environment was intoxicating. We were in Hollywood; we had a 500 seat live audience. Everything was bigger, even the furniture looked bigger, the paint was nicer, I had a dressing room that was 2000 square feet. It had three bedrooms, two reception areas and make-up room, two bathrooms and a private bedroom. Joan Rivers had that installed. What was interesting was that in the dressing room everything was small, I would say that she had the shortest toilet in the history of toilets because she was small, and then there was the crystal toilet paper holder. It was unbelievable. And any time you wanted a guest, it would be somebody big, and they want to hang out and then we had gifts for people who were on the show, it was kind of an amazing intoxicating experience.

(John Keister) And a lot of money. Just for being a writer down there, the writers got a minimum, as I remember, like five or six grand a week or something like that.

I was 30. And anyway, there was also this aspect to it that, I mean, I thought that I could eventually find myself in the business down there, but then there was being a father, a first time father and to have twin boys, that was going to be really difficult. I had been on the show for a couple of weeks and then during the Thanksgiving vacation I think, it gave me time for my head to clear and I was like, wait, I can't, I can't do this.

(Bill Stainton) I wanted to name John as the host [of Almost Live!] against everybody's wishes. I'm not sure that John knows that. I'm pretty sure I was the only person fighting for him and fortunately I won out. And it was a risky move.

(John Keister) As soon as I got back to Seattle, people came immediately and said, "You can be the host of the show." Things moved very quickly.

(Bill Stainton) I wanted somebody local, John's extremely local, I wanted somebody who had continuity with the show and I wanted somebody with an edge. The big question was that John was always the icing on the cake. What's going to happen when you make John the cake? In the first five years it was here's a John Keister bit. Now it was going to be the whole show's a John Keister bit. Until we finally figured out how to design the show around John as opposed to trying to fit John into a show that was designed around Ross.

(Jim McKenna) I was surprised when John took over. I just assumed it would be Pat (Cashman) and then John would be the rogue element.

(Bill Stainton) Season 5 was John's first year as host and I simply plugged him into the existing, 1-hour, comedy/talk format. The problem was that this was the format that evolved to showcase Ross's strengths, and John's strengths were different. Season 5 was a mess (At least, that's my recollection. I'm sure we did some really good work—at least in the comedy department—but I was so miserable I just remember the whole season as being miserable.) The interviews just weren't working. At that time it was still really hard to get decent guests to come to Seattle (we weren't quite the capital of the world yet), and John just wasn't the interviewer that Ross was.

(Dori Monson) I would agree it was really awkward at first because John was the sidekick; it was really interesting watching him transition to become a host because they were so physically different. First of all Ross looks like a television host and I would remember John would wear those garish Ted Nugent-like shirts. It was so physically different, Ross was the suit and tie guy and John was 180°. Ross was pretty slick and he'd done a lot of stand up but John became distinctive it his own way and I think that's what elevated the show. I think people identified with John a little bit more as a Seattle guy.

(Pat Cashman) John would be the first to tell you that it was a very rocky road, as he had none of the skills that Ross did, the ability to interview people and be smooth about it and comfortable on his feet. It wasn't John's deal at all.

(Steve Wilson) You can see it, you can F-ing see it! There's a great thing where he's interviewing Jerry Seinfeld and Jerry's like, what is going on? Is this a joke? Yea, he was very uncomfortable doing it. Extremely uncomfortable. And it appeared at the end of that first year that this was not going to work.

(Marty Riemer) I vividly remember this party Ross had after he'd come back from LA and he'd invited myself and John Keister, it was a very small gathering of people, and I remember John, Ross and I were talking, and this was when this was still the carry-over from Ross's format so John stepped into the roll as host, and John said he was so horribly uncomfortable hosting that show, because it was Ross's format.

(John Keister) I had interviewed people for The Rocket for years so I thought, I know how to interview people, but it's completely different interviewing people for print and just sort of hanging out in a coffee shop than it is on stage interviewing people. I didn't understand that and when the show started I was shocked that I couldn't do it very well. I was stunned watching myself, "What am I doing wrong here, what's going on?"—and then I am exhausted because I have kids and the show starts to tank and I am like, "This is great, this is great." So, I gave up a job in Hollywood and I am going to be the guy that rides this show down and that pretty much will be it, in terms of my career in TV. And the other thing is I didn't have the confidence to dress the way that I wanted to dress. I was not a clothes person. They were dressing me in suits that I wasn't comfortable with and I didn't have the confidence to say, "No, this is the way that I want to do the show," and the first year hosting that show was probably the worst year of my life. It was like, I was exhausted, the show was failing; I was doing terrible. I lost 30 pounds. I lost a tremendous amount of weight and at that time in our nation's history that was code for certain things and I found out later that there actually had been a rumor going around that I had AIDS, which of course was not true.

1988

- Washington State's Convention Center opens.
- Crack cocaine appears on the streets of America.
- The first major computer virus infects computers connected to the Internet.

1989

- The Berlin wall is torn down.
- Exxon Valdez oil spill.
- Tiananmen Square protests in China.

1990

- Nelson Mandela released from South African prison.
- Seattle hosts the Goodwill Games.
- I-90 bridge sinks.

A New Beginning

1988. They lost their host, a potentially crippling blow, and their new host is forced to step in and carry on in a format completely unsuited to his talents. He's experiencing, first-hand, Star Trek's Kobayashi Maru—the no-win scenario. Almost Live! was on the verge of paying off everyone's low-hanging punch line: Almost Dead. But little did anyone know that the next several months would hold defining moments for the show. Moments that would take the program to a level they never dreamed. The molecules in the air of local television were changing.

(Bill Stainton) We came real close to being canceled after Season 5. I spent the summer trying to fix the show. For many weeks, I tried to figure out a way to salvage the interview segments: Could I increase the guest budget and try to get better guests? Could I get coaching for John? Could I have somebody else do the interview segments while John remained the host of the show?

(Steve Wilson) So now comes the time where we're saving jobs. Our Program Director, Craig Smith, young guy, innovative guy, he wants to grow the show, he sees something there, so he says, "Why don't you guys do four shows that we can have as filler for the NBA Championships over the summer?" So John and Bill, they just pulled taped bits from the show with laugh tracks and then they had wraps in between: "Hi, it's me, John Keister, blah, blah, blah, blah, blah, here's that piece." And we came up with a few innovative ways to do these wraps in the studio. It was basically a clip show. They ran those shows after the basketball games and they held the audience. And then came time where the show's going to go or it's not going to go.

(Bill Stainton) I really considered every option. Finally, in desperation, I said to myself, "It would be so great if I could just eliminate the damn interview segments!" Well that led to a new question: What would I fill the time with? So, more options: Musical guests? More written comedy? Longer comedian segments? Nothing seemed to be either right or, if it was right, workable. Desperation again. I said to myself, "It would be so great if I didn't have to fill the damn time!"

That was the breakthrough. I started thinking about what that would look like. Obviously, we'd be talking about a half-hour show. But a half-hour show of just the stuff that we—and John—did best.

(Bill Nye) I feel that we all realized that to be successful the show would have to change completely. Bill Stainton articulated it well: In order to be successful, it would have to be an extension of John rather than an extension of Ross. The show would have to be shorter, tighter, feature comedy videos, and be driven by good writing. John being such a student of comedy, and comedy films, stepped in and led the way. Bill Stainton was a key. Despite some friction, he enabled John to be at his best.

(John Keister) The Program Director said, "Why don't you try and put together a version of the show that is a half hour long and just sort of concentrate on sketch comedy?"

(Steve Wilson) Get rid of the band, get rid of the Letterman thing; let's do Saturday Night Live. Make John do what he's good at.

(Bill Stainton) As a half-hour show, we might be able to move to a better time slot (We were still in the extremely un-funny Sunday at 6pm slot).

(Steve Wilson) So we're coming in on the season and Craig Smith says, "You know what I'm going to do, I'm going to push back Saturday Night Live," which, at that time was using all sorts of Hollywood brat packers and was going into the toilet. He said, "We're going to push Saturday Night Live back and we're going to run our show here."

(John Keister) Not an easy thing to do, but it's a lot easier if you have the president of the Affiliates Association in your station, which we did. His name was Eric Bremner, and Bremner liked me and so did Ancil Payne. I was in total awe of Ancil Paine. Really, it was like, that was the guy; I had never been more proud to work for somebody. He was a guy who stood for things. I tell you, I make jokes about the glory that was KING and stuff like that but he wasn't part of that, he led by example. He would frequently tell me that it's going to be okay, hang in there, and so they said, "We are going to ask NBC if we can push Saturday Night Live." So NBC sent back a message, You can do it for—I think it was a certain amount of time—for six weeks——and then we will see.

(Bill Stainton) Serendipitously, this was when Carson was leaving The Tonight Show, and the Leno/Letterman wars were in full swing. Affiliates were pissed at NBC, and NBC was doing everything they could to appease the affiliates—particularly the more important ones, which included KING. Under normal circumstances, we could never have bumped SNL to midnight. Lorne Michaels is very protective of his time slot! But these weren't normal circumstances. The planets aligned. Just when the half-hour format became a real possibility, so did the coveted Saturday, 11:30pm time slot.

(John Keister) What happened then was we go to do the first show and they want me to wear a suit and I am like, "I am not going through another year of this, I felt terrible on the first show, I am not doing this again,"—and so the next show I showed up in my jeans and a shirt and they were like, "Where is the suit?" I said, "No, this is the way it's going to be from now."

(Marty Riemer) The brilliant evolution came when Keister said, "Screw it, I'm throwing it all out and I'm going to do what I'm confortable with."

(Jim Sharp) It was no longer a talk show, he turned it into the show it needed to be. John didn't do a random monologue, he did a rant; he was angry, he was the underdog.

(Marty Riemer) And that transformation saved the show, that really took it to a level that no one ever expected, least of all Keister. I think he's probably thinking, I'm just doing this for survival.

(John Keister) That episode we entered for the IRIS Award won. That's the award for best local show in America. So then NBC sent a telegram to KING that said, "Looks like you made the right decision."

And so it stayed, it stayed that way and people at first were like, "Why should we have to sit through this to get to Saturday Night Live?" There were lots of complaints, which I was afraid there would be, and then it became more like, "Thank God."

(Bill Stainton) When we made the decision to go to a half hour, that was really a big deal.

(Bill Nye) It felt like we finally had the chance to take a few risks.

(Scott Schaefer) That was really when it hit its sweet spot, when they changed it to a half hour all sketch comedy show. Like most sketch comedy shows you'll have one good bit out of every five so the longer the show the more filler you need so with only a half hour you had a better chance of success.

(Steve Wilson) So we're out of the Sunday night ghetto, we're down to a half an hour and we're going to be all sketch. And the first season we were on, pretty much the letters we were getting were, "What is this? This show sucks! Where's Saturday Night Live?" The second season, "This is great!" That's when we learned how to make TV.

(John Keister) What happened then was that none of the other stations counter-programmed us because they were all running away from SNL. On KIRO they were running infomercials that people would pay 50 bucks for, and we were running half minute spots that I believe the account executives would sign for like two grand a pop and they were all ours, they were all KING's. Back then they were making a fortune off the show. I was told by the representative of a beer company that our show had the purest beer demographic of any show, local or national. What we had was basically the college crowd, the beer consumers, beer and pizza, so if you watched Almost Live! what you would see is ads for beer, ads for pizza, ads for Jeeps, ads for things that were desirable to young college-age and just after.

And then they started selling the sponsorships to Budweiser. After our first commercial break it would be, "Almost Live! is presented by Budweiser,"—and they paid, I believe a half million dollars a year for that privilege.

(Bill Stainton) Season 6 saw us as a leaner, funnier show in a golden time slot—and we never looked back. To me, Season 6 was when we really hit our stride as a local comedy show to be reckoned with.

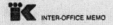

TO: John Keister   c/c   SUBJECT: Lunch re-cap

FROM: Bill Stainton

DATE: 1/13/89

Just wanted to re-cap some of the things we discussed at lunch yesterday:

1) We agree that the taped pieces need to be especially strong. I see Joe, Nancy and you as our primary taped piece producers. I am also planning on writing and producing more pieces. I see Ed and Bill N. as working more on in-studio comedy.

2) I have asked Bill N. to take responsibility for the pre-show festivities.

3) We both have concerns about Act 2. You are being held responsible for too much of the writing, which puts an undue amount of pressure on you. Also, the act has become predictable. I suggest beginning with the conclusion and working backwards. We also need to think of other elements to include to make it less predictable.

4) We decided to stop fighting the monologue. Let's do one, but we still want to look for ways to make it different. A prop of some kind is a good idea, as long as it doesn't become too much of a gimmick. Maybe something along the lines of boxes over-the-shoulder to correspond to the joke subjects.

5) I have some concern over your involvement in so many taped pieces, primarily because I believe it may interfere with other show preparation that needs to be done. I would like you to try to gear your taped piece involvement toward the beginning of the week, and leave Friday free for the writers' meeting, and for going over the show with me.

6) You and I will plan a substantial block of time next week to go over some show tapes. Please let me know what your Evening schedule is as soon as possible. I'd like to look at your performances more than general show comments.

7) I think we both agree that the show is on pretty good footing-- certainly a step above last year--but it hasn't really turned into the show we had planned on doing by now. We need to think in terms of the unpredictable to keep the show fresh.

By the way, the Mahi-mahi was really good.

Your pal,

An inter-office memo between Bill Stainton and John Keister not long after they made the jump to late night.

Oh yea, I remember that sketch!

- **Capable Woman**
  The super hero for the feminist crowd! She isn't new exactly, it's just that she's finally broken through the male-dominated super hero power structure and is just now getting the recognition that is so rightly hers.

- **The Survivalist**
  Ed Wyatt as Tex Rainer, direct from an underground bunker in Grants Pass, Oregon. Hopefully there's still enough of you alive out there to watch.

- **Training Films**
  Those incredibly useful "How to" videos like, How to hold a garage sale, How to get a job, How guys barbeque.

- **Guide to Living in Seattle, Parts 1-5**
  Wake to the sound of glass being recycled, climb out from under your goose down comforter, put on your Gore-Tex, fire up your home espresso machine, enjoy your left over Thai take out from last night before hopping in your car to share the road with bicyclists.

- **The Last Northwesterner**
  The Californians have taken over. Even Dick's Drive In has been renamed Dudes. John Keister makes a desperate run for the border, taking with him the last vestiges of our culture.

Coming and Going

With the shift to a new format, new time-slot and new host, the cast went through changes as well. Familiar faces left and fresh, new talent came on board. The show's foundation had been laid but the chemistry was still working itself out.

(Joe Guppy) Ross had left to take the Late Show after Joan Rivers and Scott Schaefer tells me Not Necessarily the News on HBO is re-staffing. I had an opportunity to go to LA.

(Nancy Guppy) Joe was really good at deadpan reporter kind of stuff, which is perfect for Not Necessarily the News. He sent them a tape, they loved it, they flew him down a couple of times and he eventually became one of the reporters on the show. Then they agreed for some reason to hire us as a writing team. I think they thought they'd be able to get two for one, but it turns out it was a Writer's Guild show, a union show, and the Guild said, "No, you have to pay for both." For some reason they agreed to it and ponied up.

(Joe Guppy) It was a Writer's Guild job, a union job, obviously good money I just couldn't turn it down.

(Nancy Guppy) So we went down there with a job, we got an agent; it was the perfect way to go to LA if you're going to go to LA. And we got paid great! That's the thing with LA, we ended up writing for several different shows; most of them completely horrible and forgettable, but you make really great money. But you also work on really bad stuff. We didn't get to the level of the Seinfelds or the Simpsons; I don't know if we ever had the chops for that.

(Joe Guppy) We were only on [Not Necessarily the News] for a short stint. Thirteen weeks I think. It got us a toehold at least and then we moved around from job to job down there.

(Nancy Guppy) We ended up staying down there for three years. '89-'92.

(Ed Wyatt) I joined that cast only because a couple of the writers went with Ross to LA so they opened up a writers slot, and that's what I applied for, I didn't know I was going to be acting. I was a bit of a ham but had no acting skills. Even to this day my wife tells me I'm the worst actor in the world. After my first year Joe and Nancy went to LA to work on a show called Not Necessarily the News. That was 1989 and that was when Bob Nelson got hired. He'd been sending stuff to Bill Stainton. Bill was always getting stuff from people who fancied themselves as writers but Bob's stuff was so good he had to hire him.

(Bob Nelson) I was working in advertising at the Seattle Times and saw this local comedy show on. I'd written and performed humor in college, but it'd been about 10 years since I'd taken a crack at it, and I thought, Well, maybe they'll have an opening some day. So I wrote a bunch of sketches and brought them over to KING-TV on my lunch hour and threw the sketches on the receptionist's desk and ran away. Bill Stainton, the producer, called me the next day and told me he liked the sketches but he just hired Ed Wyatt for that year, but to keep in touch. Then I saw an article saying Joe and Nancy Guppy were leaving the following year so I wrote some more sketches, in the summer of '99, and he called me up and that's how I got on.

(Steve Wilson) What you'd get is this huge group of people who think they're funny. They say, "I'm really funny at parties; I should be on your show." The filter there would be, write ten funny sketches. Or just write five that we could use on the air. Well none of them could do it. "What do you mean write? No, I'm just funny." You had to be a writer, and you had to know how to write for television and then you had to write stuff that was really funny.

(Ed Wyatt) I wasn't a full-fledged sketch writer but I had a lot of ideas stemming back to a book I wrote at Stanford called "How to College". So that first year I wrote a lot of jokes for the monologue. I was also on camera from the very beginning because they needed people; that was part of the deal, you had to be on camera. I think my first sketch was called Dumb Guns, which was a Joe Guppy spoof on Young Guns, the movie that was basically a bunch of guys with guns in a circle shooting so that we all shot each other. There wasn't enough money to hire actors. That's how a lot of the people around the station got roped into being performers; you'd just go up to a guy in sales and say, "Hey, do you want to play a part in this sketch?" This was in those freewheeling days when everybody had a bottle of whiskey in their top drawer and you'd just run around asking people to be in your sketch and it was no problem. We were always co-opting people from around the station and some of them were great, that's how Tracey [Conway] came on board, she was a receptionist with a great acting background and we went, "Oh, this girl's really good,"—and the next thing you know she's a cast member.

(Bob Nelson) I think my first contract was for six weeks with an option through the end of the year. It took two or three years before we really built it up to full time status, about the time we were on Comedy Central. During my first summer I actually went back to the Seattle Times in the advertising division and worked there and that got me through the first couple of years. The first year [on

Almost Live!] it was $300 a week for 30 weeks so that was $9000 a year gross. The nice thing is that we didn't pay a lot of taxes.

(Tracey Conway) I started being pulled into sketches here and there in '89. I didn't start as a full writer/performer until the fall of '90. At first they would pull me in when they needed a woman who could say quite a few lines and that they knew they could count on to deliver. I was an actual actor who was working at KING to pay the rent, so when they found out I really had a history, that I was trained; it was like, "Oh yea, go see if you can get that girl in HR." So in '90 things are really starting to gel for the show. They'd just hired Bob, but, hey, sometimes you gotta have a woman, they needed a wife once in a while, or a female executive. It was just the kind of thing where it would be ridiculous never to have a woman around. It wasn't their intention not to, but I think Bill had a budget for Nye, Wyatt, Keister, Nelson and Stainton. It was essentially those five guys plus their shooter. Wilson and Cashman were already full-time KING employees.

(Bob Nelson) Even when I first started and was making no money it's hard to believe you get to go in and meet like-minded people and go out and shoot things. I got to do exactly what I wanted. I've often said working at Almost Live! didn't feel like a job. Those 10 years were a little miracle in my work life.

The Prank that Failed

You've heard the line before: "It's funny until it isn't." Almost Live! got to live that out to the Nth degree. There are bad ideas and then there are bad ideas that risk lives. On April 1st, 1989, Almost Live! pulled a prank that became national news. And not in a good way. The prank? A fake news story that the Space Needle had collapsed. Orson Wells promptly pirouetted in his grave. But in the end the cast and crew learned that, in typical show biz fashion, there's no such thing as bad publicity.

(John Keister) It was April 1st and there had been a big tradition when I was editor of the University of Washington newspaper that on April 1st we would always do this cover of The Daily that would be some fake story and the whole idea was to make it as plausible as possible to freak people out as much as possible. So I was remembering that and there was a term that went around Seattle media that was, like, "Don't bother me, unless you are sure the Space Needle's falling down." That was a term that people used to use all the time. "I am going on a vacation and I don't want to get a call unless the Space Needle fell down."

(Tracey Conway) Stainton had come down to me and said, "Hi, we're going to do a spoof where we pretend that the Space Needle collapses." He said, "We're going to do it live, we're doing a live show on April 1st and we're going to fake break-in like it's breaking news and cut to the news room and have an actor who looks like a fill-in news anchor breaking the story. And then we need to cut to someone on the street who was a witness, who saw it go down, so I'm looking for somebody that our audience won't recognize." He said, "Would you do that?" I said, "Sure!"

(John Keister) We had a show that came on April 1st and it was live, we just happened to have the slot, I forget what was going on that night and the network had a space.

(Steve Wilson) Since it was a special we did it live. We did not tape the show. We're going to go on the air with this first bit. We put on screen, April 1st, 1989. April Fools Day, in big type on screen.

(Bill Stainton) I wrote the bit, I edited the bit, brought in all the footage of the Space Needle being built. And we made a point of saying nobody was injured.

(Ed Wyatt) I think this was in that time when we didn't know how big we were. That we thought, it was just, you know, we're Almost Live!, no one gives a rat's ass, we'll put this on, it'll be a funny little piece.

(Jeff Renner) I thought [the sketch] was a little bit over the top. I think you can have a lot of fun if you really identify it clearly, then that might not be totally inappropriate. But that was a little bit too close to reality, and we got a lot of blow back on that. That was probably one of the skits I was less fond of.

(Bill Stainton) I ran the script—that's the one thing I did well, the only reason I kept my job—I ran the script by the three people above me. And they all approved the script so I'd covered my ass, but they never saw the finished piece. Typical of us I probably finished editing it an hour before the show. We had April Fools Day on the screen, which frankly, I didn't want to do. I thought, C'mon, that's gonna ruin it!

(John Keister) When we ran it by the Program Director, he said, "Okay, fine but you've got to put April Fools Day on it," and I said, "Well, if we do that, why even do it?" But he was like, "No, you've got to do that," and we were like, "Well, whatever."

(Nancy Guppy) We were furious that we had to put April Fools on screen.

(Bill Stainton) My greatest hope was that maybe a few people might look out their windows and go, "Okay, they got us." The segment runs. It's in act one.

(Ed Wyatt) Two things we did wrong, well, among many things, first, we hired that actor to play the news guy. So instead of it being Bill Nye or me or Keister it was a guy that no one had seen before, it was a hired actor. That's the first mistake. And then the other thing was the image of the Needle being collapsed. Those guys did a fantastic job with it. I do recall looking at that image and someone saying, "Wow, that's pretty good, is that too good?"

(Tracey) So, of course, if you just sort of heard, breaking news, we interrupt our regular scheduled programing for a news bulletin, and then they cut to me having this reaction...

(John Keister) Tracey is a trained actress, she looked really horrified and it was really her performance I think that kicked it in.

(Steve Wilson) So we air the bit and people just tuning in, expecting to see Lifestyles of the Rich and Famous, see this and they freak and they run from their TVs to start calling. So John does his monologue and the phone in the booth starts ringing. We go to break, I've got two minutes and thirty seconds to get ready for the next bit and I pick up the phone. It's the switchboard. The first thing I hear is, "What have you guys done? We've got, like, four hundred phone calls about the Space Needle falling over." And I'm thinking, Oh (bleep).

(Bill Stainton) During the commercial break our front desk operator runs into the studio and hands me this note telling me that we've shut down the 911 lines. I mean, not only have we shut down KING's switchboard but also the Space Needle's switchboard and we shut down the 911 lines. We overloaded the 911 lines in western Washington. I'm like, "Oh (bleep)."

(Steve Wilson) We've got a camera outside so I said, "Swing the camera around to shoot the Space Needle." John comes on the air and says, "We've got our live camera out there, see, still standing, everything's fine, it's just a joke, it's April Fools Day."

(John Keister) And so we took a shot of it and I went, "Look, it's there, it's no problem," but I didn't have any idea of how crazy things had gotten, and so after the show I got in a cab and I went to host the Seattle comedy competition. I went directly from the studio out of the building, so I didn't know about what was going on. The rest of the cast was left to deal with it and then when I got home, I have a lot of friends in the media and there are these messages: "What did you do?" "What have you done?" And the next day I looked at the front page, I go through the papers and go, "Oh my god!"

(Steve Wilson) Next day, oh my god. Sunday, Monday it was in papers all over.

(Bill Stainton) The next day, Sunday, I spent most of the day on the phone with the Space Needle and their lawyers. They were going to sue me, personally, they were going to sue KING-TV;

they were probably going to sue NBC. The Space Needle people were just furious with us, saying, at least you could have given us a heads up.

(Pat Cashman) I wasn't involved with it, but I remember thinking, Really? This isn't a good idea. But it kind of turned out to be, in some ways, a turning point for the show; we got some national attention and stuff like that so you could say that that was good.

(John Keister) When I went in, of course everybody was summoned into this big meeting room and we were told that it shut the 911-system down so that people with legitimate emergencies couldn't call in.

(Bill Stainton) Monday, we're front-page news all across the country. This is front-page news, above the fold, in every major paper across the country. And then I get a call from the people at the Needle, the same people who were trying to sue me the day before, now they're saying, "How can we milk this?" Because it was the most publicity the Space Needle had had since the day it was built. So we apologized. I mean, we're a comedy show, we hurt people's feelings all the time, but this time we actually put lives in danger by shutting down the 911 lines. We really did F up.

(Tracey Conway) So that was my debut on Almost Live!. And the show was almost cancelled.

(Dr. Pepper Schwartz) That's the edginess of comedy. You're going to occasionally go too far. There's risk. It's a blood sport.

(Nancy Guppy) Of course, in retrospect we were complete idiots. But they didn't fire us!

(John Keister) I did apologize on the air for it, but it was one of those things, it was before any of the big horrific big terrorist acts that had been perpetrated in the United States but there was this moment in my life where I couldn't believe how much trouble I was in. I mean, I was like, "Am I going to do time over this? What's going to happen?"

(Bill Stainton) Post 9/11 we would never do something like that now. Actually, now, because of us, there's now federal law that you can't do it.

(Bill Nye) The whole story blew over after a while. After all, the Space Needle is pretty tall, and easily noticed. It was obviously still standing. I believe it still is.

(John Keister) The news department was furious, so there is a lot of things that were really bad, but when I look back on it I am actually very proud of it because I am a lot more reticent to do crazy things as I have gotten older and more cautious and raised kids and done all this sort of stuff and I would never do something like that today because I would be in GITMO. I mean, I wouldn't do anything like that but when I look back on it, there was a time in my life when I actually had the guts to do something like that, that I was strong enough to push the Space Needle. It really taught me a lesson. It was before the Internet and before all that sort of stuff but the power we had, that the station had, I don't think anybody at the station understood how much power we really did have until that moment, it was so shocking the reaction that we got. It was something I will never forget, it's unbelievable.

INTER-OFFICE MEMO

TO: Almost Live Staff c/c   SUBJECT: Live show

FROM: Your pal, Bill

DATE: 3/1/89

    In order to get some idea of what the show would do if, and
I repeat, <u>if</u>, we were to move to Saturday as an airdate, we're
going to try one (with Entertainment This Week as our lead-in).
The April 1st show will be done live at 7:00 p.m. This is a
Saturday. Actually, our schedule doesn't really change all that
much. This could be a real good opportunity for some exposure
for Almost Live, so let's really give it our all. We should
plan on taking advantage of the fact that 1: it's April Fool's
Day, and 2: we're live.
        Please start thinking of ideas now. Thanks.

Inter-office memo before the prank.

INTER-OFFICE MEMO

TO: KING 5 Television Staff c/c   SUBJECT: Almost Live
Space Needle Story

FROM: Sturges Dorrance

DATE: April 7, 1989

You are all aware of what happened last Saturday evening. Almost
Live staged a simulated news story about the collapse of the Space
Needle. What happened wasn't one bit funny. The furor is just now
dying down.

Hundreds of viewers misunderstood the bit, and many were genuinely
alarmed. I have talked with Bill Stainton and John Keister. Both
have acknowledged this was a serious situation. Both have apologized
publicly - as has Craig Smith and KING 5 Television.

Almost Live has been on our air four years. During that time it has
presented many hours of good television and has won numerous awards.
Saturday was a low point, but I have confidence the program will
recover from this incident.

News simulation will not, however, be part of that recovery. In
fact, there is no occasion when the credibility of our news
presentation should be jeopardized by parody or simulation - period.

SDD/mn

Inter-office memo after the prank.

Oh yea, I remember that sketch!

- **This Here Place**
  Pat Cashman as host Bob Bobbins sharing handy home repair tips with the "help" of Ralph and Larry.
- **Refrigerator Magnet Theater**
  Fridge magnets with faces talk amongst themselves while holding up photos and recipes. The drama!
- **Pike or Pine**
  The game show that asks the question every person in Seattle has asked at one time or another.
- **How Seattle are You?**
  The game show that separates the long-time natives from the late-coming transplants. Solve this equation: Four shots of regular, plus two shots of decaf, plus a sixteen ounce cup filled with skim milk minus all foam equals what? The answer: A quadruple half-caf skinny dry grande.
- **The Ballard Files**
  Ya sure, the truth is out there, you betcha.
- **DJ Randy Scott--Cop/Waiter/Pilot/Dentist**
  Randy Scott, Seattle's top part-time disc jockey, at work during his other jobs, yet still sounding like an overly caffeinated AM DJ.
- **Politically Correct Seattle**
  How to offend nobody. Who knew the word "Fruitcake" was offensive in so many ways?

There are certain subjects that are untouchable, and Almost Live! found out what one of them was. A seemingly harmless sketch nearly gets the show cancelled and the entire cast and crew fired. Their crime? They made fun of cars. More specifically, American cars. What made it such an unforgivable sin (in management's eyes) was due to what one of KING's other local programs had done earlier.

What I found most interesting about these interviews was the amount of bitterness many of the cast still holds all these years later. Managers take heed: Give your employees the red ass and they're like elephants—they never forget.

(Bill Stainton) For the most part KING completely left us alone. Even after we knocked over the Space Needle, still, I was the last person who saw what was going on the air. The only time we really got in trouble, and they almost cancelled the show, was when we did this live piece making fun of car dealers. That was a really unpleasant meeting.

You don't mess with Jean Enersen and you didn't mess with the car dealers.

(Bob Nelson) Evening Magazine had done a story previously about how to get the best deal at a car dealership and it talked about all the tricks they use when you go in to avoid. They'd gotten in a lot of trouble for that.

(John Keister) The car dealers went nuts. They organized a boycott of KING.

(Steve Wilson) The car dealers in Washington bought, like, a million dollars worth of time and they just pulled it.

(John Keister) This was a real financial blow to KING.

(Rick Blangiardi) What I remember is that I was new to Seattle and we had a market-wide cancelation by the car guys (dealerships), they were so organized. Some guy I'd never heard of before said he was representing all the dealerships and he said, "Kiss your car business goodbye." And sure enough they all followed up. It was real and it was significant.

(Bob Nelson) I'm not sure how long after that, but then we did a sketch about American cars, which were pretty bad at that time. And it was basically saying the quality wasn't that good but they were trying to get better.

(John Keister) Okay, so the sketch was not the cure for cancer. In fact it was kind of a time-filler for us. It wasn't one that people would list on their top 10 Almost Live! bits.

(Rick Blangiardi) Automotive category is typically a top three advertiser in television stations and that's a lot of money and not a situation we could sustain from the standpoint of, okay, that's just the way it is, I'll go on to the next thing.

(Bill Stainton) It was a valid point. Car dealers are the life-blood of a TV station because they spend the most for ads, unless it's a political season. So, okay, that's a legitimate point. Let's have a meeting with the general manger and the sales director and talk about how much damage was done.

(Bob Nelson) So the next Tuesday when we came in we were called on the carpet by the General Manager, Rick Blangiardi. And for some reason the News Director, Bob Jordan was in the meeting. And those guys read us the riot act.

(Steve Wilson) Bob Jordan, who was the News Director, was furious with us and Blangiardi stood back and let him go after us.

(Bill Stainton) Bad meeting doesn't come close. There was no excuse for that meeting. I wish I could turn back time; I would have done things differently then. Basically it was, let's bring the Almost Live! cast in and scream at them. Rick was saying that he was going to fire us, when he saw that on the air his first instinct was to immediately cancel the show and fire all of us. And Bob Jordan just starts going into us. And we're thinking, Why the F are you even here, you're the goddamn News Director; this has nothing to do with you. It was like, let's humiliate the cast.

(Tracey Conway) I'd never had parents who yelled at me. I'm surprised I didn't have a cardiac arrest at that table because I was so scared. I'd never been talked to like that.

(Bob Nelson) They were screaming at us and going around the table and asking us each individually, "What the hell were you thinking? What were you thinking Ed? What were you thinking Bob? What were you thinking John?" I think all of us thought if we said the wrong thing that the show could be cancelled. It felt like, even if you wanted to talk back to them that you'd be endangering the show.

(Ed Wyatt) I remember muttering under my breath something like, "Mellow out, dude." Steve Wilson, I think, laughed, but nobody else heard it and I certainly didn't have the cojones to say it out loud. I think we were all kind of shell-shocked, especially because it wasn't exactly the type of piece you'd defend - it was a last-minute bit we needed to fill out the show.

(John Keister) Blangiardi went around the room and asked everybody individually, "Are you aware that we are under this boycott from car dealers?" And they would say, "Yes," but then he would stop, and then he would go down the line asking, "Are you aware...?" He allowed people to say, yes, and not let them say another word. And then he says, "Okay, I am glad, you know; it's interesting to me that you all understand this so then I can ask you..." and then he starts screaming, "What the F were you thinking?" He starts pounding on the table. It was like a football coach chewing out a team that hadn't performed the way he wanted to on the field. Blangiardi had in fact been a Division 1 football coach. He had a photo of him and Vince Lombardi prominently displayed in his office. Maybe a football team would have responded correctly, the problem was we were not a football team.

(Rick Blangiardi) I remember being on bended knee, if you will, going out to these dealerships. I drove around all the way up through Bellingham and down to Tacoma and everywhere else and meeting with these car guys one on one, apologizing to them and asking for their business back. While I'm not above doing that it was a very unnecessary thing doing that. I'm new to the town and I've got a real challenge on my hands with this and these guys [Almost Live!] weren't making it easier with these antics and I thought there should be some responsibility here and some sensitivity.

(John Keister) He was very angry and that was a really F-ed up meeting, but Blangiardi was a real straight shooter. A different GM probably would have fired us.

(Pat Cashman) I wasn't [at the meeting] but I heard about it. It sounded like it was kind of an unreasonable over-the-top scolding, (but) this is what comedy shows do, they make fun of stuff and we don't want to feel like now we've got to be so careful the rest of the time because we don't want to offend anybody or any potential advertiser.

(Steve Wilson) They said, "You cannot pick on any clients we have, you cannot pick on our newscasters." They made a list of people we couldn't touch now. And the car joke was pretty innocuous. It didn't say anything about the car dealers, it was joking about the cars, which were crap anyway, everybody knew it; it was in the news.

(Bill Stainton) So during this meeting about the car thing all of a sudden Bob Jordan just leans across the desk and puts his finger in my chest and screams, "Keep you goddamn hands out of my news library!"

(Steve Wilson) We couldn't use any footage anymore, no more news footage, which cut us back considerably.

(Bill Stainton) We had to use news footage all the time for the John Report and other sketches. We always had this agreement, fine, we could use the footage. But Bob Jordan was like, "No, you can't keep news footage."

(John Keister) There was a point where I could see that Blangiardi understood things had gone too far.

(Steve Wilson) But a deal that we struck was that we could use stills from their newscasts. We could use stills as long as we made them black and white. So if we needed a shot of the Governor instead of going into the news library and getting footage we would have to grab a still and make it black and white.

(Bill Stainton) I really kind of wish that I'd quit right then. I thought, This is just a joke.

(Steve Wilson) Soon after, the I-90 Bridge sank and we needed a clip. But, there was no law that said we couldn't get it from another station so we got some footage from KIRO and used that.

(Bill Stainton) And I put a big credit up there, footage courtesy of KIRO-TV.

(Steve Wilson) Of course then Bob comes unglued, "I thought I told you to stay out of our library!" And I said, "I did, I got that from someone else." I basically did an end-around.

(Pat Cashman) I think what most of us were afraid of is that now we're going to have to give approval of the show before it ever goes on the air. The fact of the matter is, for the most part, nobody watched the show before it went on the air, it just went on the air, we record it and it's on the air, nobody looked at it. So, for that one standout moment to occur in 15 years is, in the long view, not a big deal; that's actually pretty amazing when you think about it. It's always the one you don't see coming that wind ups offending somebody.

(John Keister) Blangiardi asked me afterwards, he sort of pulled me aside, and he goes, "How do you think, how did that go?" I said, "Well, Rick, you know, I think I understood what you were trying to do but I don't think that went very well."

(Bob Nelson) My thoughts on that meeting were that they perhaps had a right to have a meeting and say, "You know, you guys knew about Evening Magazine, why didn't you ask us before you did this?" My whole problem with that meeting was their whole demeanor. It was the least professional behavior I've ever seen from management in the 40 years I've been working now.

(John Keister) I would say in his defense he [Blangiardi] was honest, he was an honest person, but he made a major error in treating a creative team like a football team. That was a major error that a lot of people I know never forgave him for. And then none of the car dealers gave a crap about it. They didn't care.

(Bill Stainton) But we didn't get fired. What's funny is we all outlasted them.

Oh yea, I remember that sketch!

- **Studs from Microsoft**
  Two women go out on dates with Studs John, Bill and Ed. The women were not amused. Memorable line from Stud Bill: "I just want to see a bra up close. A real one."

- **Lynnwood Beauty Academy**
  Learn how to create the Poofed hair, the Big Scary Hair, and the Lynnwood patented Wall-a-Bangs. Also, how to put on make up using the trowel method of application.

- **Enumclaw Movie Reviews**
  Viewers think a few car chases or explosions would make Malcolm X a much better cinematic experience.

- **The John Report/The Late Report**
  A news report with punch lines. Such as...
  A woman at a boys and girls charity auction paid $1000 for a poker party with Governor Mike Lowry. However, the auction received no bids for a game of Twister with Wayne Cody.

- **The Condom Store**
  A nervous customer is embarrassed to buy a condom in a store that only sells condoms.

- **Vanishing Seattle**
  Things that are becoming more and more rare, such as the amazing street corner with no espresso cart, or the man who has never eaten Thai food.

1991

- The Gulf War ends.
- Freddie Mercury dies of AIDS.
- Nirvana's Nevermind released.
- The world notices Seattle.

Seattle in the Spotlight

It's hard to pinpoint exactly when Seattle exploded. It would be easy to say it was on September 24th, 1991, the day Nirvana's album Nevermind was released. That was certainly one of the factors, the grunge thing. But there were multiple events that contributed to Seattle being thrust into the national spotlight and Almost Live! was right there to take full advantage of them. The dominos were falling. The culture in Seattle was going through a seismic shift. Again, the timing couldn't have been more perfect.

(Tracey Conway) Seattle just exploded in the early '90s. It became *the* city in the nation. We had the music, we had the coffee, we had the software. We had the nation's interest; we were the cool city.

(Dr. John Findlay) It was like a whole national coming out party.

(Feliks Banel) The quickest way to understand how this culture changed during that really heady period—you couldn't have picked a better time for a sketch comedy show to cover Seattle's changes—Sub Pop comes out, Howard Schultz buys Starbucks—all these huge cultural changes that we're living through were all getting started right about then. Back in the '80s Seattle was almost completely ignored and then the '90s hit and Almost Live! helps keep things humble so we don't get our heads too big.

The monologues were so topical. Carson was doing that on a national level on the Tonight Show and here we had Keister doing it on a local level here and that was so necessary.

(Bob Nelson) You couldn't pick a better time to make a satirical show about Seattle. During that time Seattle was trying to grow up, which is kind of hilarious. It's like watching a teenager try to take on adult airs; Seattle was kind of the same way. There was this decision to go from being this kind of isolated, fairly big town up in the Northwest where people didn't think about you much, and there were a bunch of people in Seattle who wanted to put it on the map, so they had these grand plans for Seattle to become this metropolitan area and so we were able to ride on that. Then all these big companies took off and we had the music explosion. I'm not sure Almost Live! would have made it during another time.

(Ed Wyatt) If you look at the synergy of what was happening in Seattle, Nirvana had just released Nevermind, the Huskies were number one in the country, the Sonics were good, and we sort of tapped into that music, sports thing. John would open the show, "How about those Huskies?" and the crowd would go nuts.

(Norm Rice) The very nature of my getting elected said there was a culture change. First African American ever elected. There was just a current of excitement. We started seeing a city that was seeing itself moving forward with opportunity and growth and development. The economy started moving, downtown started growing, the bus tunnel, there was just a lot of development and a lot of positive activity. Neighborhoods were planning for their own futures; it was an exciting time.

(Pat Cashman) It was really in some ways the perfect time to be doing a show like that because there were so many new things to talk about at the time.

(Tony Ventrella) Timing is huge in the television business; it's enormous.

(Bill Stainton) The mid-'90s was when we really hit our prime and that's also when Nirvana, Pearl Jam, Soundgarden, Alice in Chains, you had Sleepless in Seattle, you had Twin Peaks, you had Northern Exposure, Microsoft, Amazon, Starbucks. All of a sudden Seattle is London in the '60s. I mean, it's the hottest spot on the planet.

(Dori Monson) I think that was the other thing that made Almost Live! the perfect show for its time. The cooler and hipper you are perceived to be the riper you are to be taken down and to be made fun of. It was a perfect confluence of events.

(Norm Rice) Before this I think people thought of Seattle as this sleepy place that had the World's Fair, but not much more, then suddenly it became, "Wow, look what's happening in Seattle! What's happening?" I used to kid people and say, "It's the water." We were in the news; we were up front and out there. It was a fun place to be.

(Joe Guppy) I remember way back in the day when I was in my comedy group, and we were pretty successful at a local theater level, and one of my fellow comedians complaining about Seattle being tiny-town and you can't get any attention here and you can't get a break. And then it proceeded to change radically. When we were in LA and we walked into a record store and we're like, "Nirvana, wait a second, Pearl Jam, hold on a second." We're in

LA and all of a sudden Seattle is like the IT town. It kind of cracked me up.

(Bill Stainton) Seattle became the capitol of the universe, but it was a double-edged sword. It made it increasingly more difficult for us to write because our strength was being able to make fun of individual neighborhoods. You know, Fremont is this, Ballard is this, and Bellevue is this. All of a sudden Microsoft money came in and money has a tendency to homogenize everything and so Ballard is Fremont is Bellevue is...not Kent, Kent is always going to be Kent...but how are you going to make fun of things if everything is a Pottery Barn?

(John Keister) I think it's unfortunate that there were lot of things that were taken away that I really miss. It's a double-edged sword, you have a lot more cultural activities, you have these new performance spaces and new restaurants and bars and all this other stuff because of this influx of people but you lose the culture and the neighborhood identity that Seattle used to have during the heart of the show and I miss that.

It's no coincidence that Almost Live!'s popularity coincided with Seattle's. The culture change provided ripe material. Particularly the music. In the early to mid-'90s Seattle's music scene was going thermal-nuclear and a few of Seattle's music insiders witnessed it up-close. Here's what they remember from those heady days before flannel shirts, torn jeans and Doc Martens started appearing in Sears catalogues as "the grunge look". And speaking of Doc Martens— Soundgarden guitarist Kim Thayil is convinced he knows how the whole Doc Marten mystique got started. Two words: Employee discount.

(Jeff Gilbert) The term *grunge* came from Meagan Jasper over at Sub Pop. She was the one who coined the phrase in reference to the inside of a dirty bong. And it was to a rock journalist and that's where that phrase caught and stuck and took off. Nobody knew it would explode the way it did, but locally, man, it was a blast.

(Kim Thayil) We weren't surprised that we had success and we weren't surprised that our friends had success because we'd been working pretty hard over a number of years. We (Soundgarden) formed in '84 and our biggest success happened ten years later in '94. Nirvana was around a shorter period of time and so was Pearl Jam, but these were good bands. They made records, they'd signed to a major label and toured around the world so they were working towards being recognized and their music heard on the radio. It wasn't that we were successful, it was the nature of the success, the fact that it was a pop culture phenomenon that was much huger than anyone could have expected that sort of crossed over to things like fashion, film and TV. And I think, perhaps it's because of the geographic identity of the whole movement that it made it easy for people in New York and London and LA to file and reference by saying, "Hey, there's this thing in Seattle. The Seattle sound, or some guy called it grunge, let's call it grunge because it's alliterative with Punk," and all this other stuff.

(Jeff Gilbert) The local musicians were not pleased at all when the whole grunge look became a thing. The way they dressed was very organic in the first place. Nobody could afford nice clothes and nobody would wear them if you did. It was all about flannel and jeans, however ragged, and the Doc Marten boots which were all weather, all-purpose. The metal guys would wear their white tennis shoes while the grunge guys always wore Doc Martens. That's how you could tell who was who because all the guys in all the bands had super, super long hair.

(Joleen Winther Hughes) It was weird to see. You know we watched MTV and all of a sudden you'd have all these people in plaid and boots and just the look and so people would take the look as what it was, not the heart and soul behind the music. Nothing was ever meant to be a fashion statement.

(Kim Thayil) This is what's so weird about the whole grunge thing, the fact that the normal ripped up jeans and surplus boots you wore would become these weird designer elements. That it would become a fashion thing for people in Europe or New York. That was one of the more obnoxious things about Seattle becoming really huge. It made it seem like so much of this was a fad or a trend. This is the way we pretty much dressed in high school or college; it hadn't changed. These things were just basic attire and all of sudden they made it look like it was some sort of fad.

I never owned a pair of Doc Martens. No, what people wore were Army surplus combat boots because they were really cheap to get. They were solid and they were black. I wore combat boots before the band even formed. Our manager, Susan [Silver] worked at a designer shoe store, and I think it was called John Fluevog? Does that sound familiar? I think she worked at a store near Pike Place Market and they sold Doc Martens and that's why Chris [Cornell—Soundgarden's lead singer] had a pair of Doc Martens, because his girlfriend/wife (Susan Silver) worked at a store that sold them so he probably got a discount on them! Because otherwise people didn't wear damn Doc Martens because they were too expensive, unless it was some rich kid from the suburbs. That's what I'm trying to say, people didn't wear that crap. I guess if you're in New York or LA and work for some rock magazine or MTV you probably wear Doc Martens and probably think, "Oh, those Seattle guys wear Doc Martens!" What? This isn't LA or New York. That's probably how that started, because every time I see that, it's like, "Wait, the only person I know that wore those was Chris and…ohhhh."

(Jeff Gilbert) The weather was so crap-tacular around here and dreary—that was a whole social structure—so they would get together and practice, not thinking it would go anywhere, just to make noise and write songs and drink a heck of a lot of beer and occasionally do a few shows with other bands, and that would become a party, and that's how the scene really became to germinate. But mostly it was a lot of bored people up here, because what do you do when you've got super long hair as a dude and you're dressed like a lumberjack? You'd go to a concert when you could afford it, but the clubs are where everybody went because they were free or very, very cheap.

Everybody got into and dug what everybody else was doing. The grunge guys thought it was amazing that Queensryche was selling platinum records, and Heart before them. It's funny, Alice in Chains was considered a hair band for a very long time but they were far too talented to be put in that category. If you want to find the missing link between grunge and metal, it's going to be Alice in Chains. When they started out they were a glam band, full on make up and brushed up hair and then at one point they morphed, and when they did it changed everything.

(Joleen Winther Hughes) Before I was at RCKCNDY I was a music promoter. I worked for Soundgarden and Alice in Chains and Pearl Jam and the Screaming Trees. It was really weird the first time we started hearing everything on the radio, like, wherever you would go. It was just a weird thing where something that was yours in your community and people that you hang out with and had a beer with or walked down the street or rented your apartment or sold your washer and dryer to, you know they are just like your friends, right? These are just your friends and then, now they're famous.

(Jeff Gilbert) We didn't realize it was beginning to take off nationally. But around home here it was so exciting. On any given night of the week, even if there wasn't a show at a club, there was a party to go to. Every night it was like, "Where do we go to see who's playing and how do we get as much beer as possible?" The Central used to sell one-dollar cans of 16 ounce Schmidt animal beer, and then the Off Ramp used to offer Hash After the Bash, which means at closing time in order to meet the requirements of their liquor license they had to sell a certain amount of food in proportion to alcohol, which was the law back then. So after they shut down the music they would offer for about a half an hour Hash After the Bash, which was fifty cents, and everybody in all of

Seattle, all the musicians, all the party people would end up at the Off Ramp and get a paper plate and a plastic fork, it was like an army soup line, and they'd just splatter a ladle full of scrambled eggs and hash browns and you could eat your fill, but you only had 30 minutes to do it. And there was no part of the scene that was polarized, everybody just showed up there. It was like a ritual every Friday and Saturday night.

(Joleen Winther Hughes) Nowadays with social media and with everything being so instantaneous, trends just instantly come and go. At the time we were still dealing with publication deadlines. People didn't carry mobile phones and they were too expensive at that time. I think we had one computer for the whole office and there was no Internet. It was all very snail pace. So it took a while for everything to catch on, so when it did, you know, you're just living and going to your apartment and you're going to work and doing your thing every day just like you probably do today, and just all of a sudden the focus is on it. So it's almost like nobody understood what it meant to be famous or what that responsibility was or that there was a responsibility with it.

(Jeff Gilbert) There were some new bands, Supersuckers being one of them, that moved here thinking this is the new Athens, Georgia, that gave birth to REM and the B-52s. It started to happen here and people started moving here to get caught up in the inertia of the scene.

(Joleen Winther Hughes) I got to the point where I couldn't listen to demo tapes because they were all Pearl Jam clones, I mean every single is a Pearl Jam clone. And of course nobody in Seattle really likes Stone Temple Pilots or Creed because they were Pearl Jam clones.

(Jeff Gilbert) Every night for years it was so exciting around here. Never a dull moment. I don't even recall watching TV for several years because I was always out, every single night. And you could roll up anywhere, the Gorilla Gardens or Squid Row up on Capitol Hill and that's where you'd see bands like L7. Some of these places you'd have to wipe your shoes off *after* you left the place. At the Central their toilets would constantly overflow and there'd just be a film of piss-water all over the floor. It was fun.

(Joleen Winther Hughes) I feel the same way. It's like I don't remember watching TV during that time either because I was out every single night. I mean I would be at RKCNDY then go to the Weathered Wall and be down at the Colourbox and be maybe at the Central and then maybe go back to RKCNDY. I mean it was not just one night; it's almost probably every weekend night and possibly two or three nights on the weekdays and that was normal.

(Kim Thayil) It was a fun thing to do to go hang out with a bunch of friends and watch your peers perform and check out their new material, so there was always something to do: daily socializing and beer drinking and listening to music.

(Chris Ballew) That was really the case. We took the stage with nobody knowing who we were on a Tuesday night and it was packed, and bam, we won over a crowd. One of the reasons we were able to find a foothold was that people went out to see live music like crazy because they were all excited to see the next big thing. It was great. You had an audience no matter what. One time we decided to see how many times we could play. I remember we played 15 times in one month and the crowds just got bigger and bigger. They were all out there anyway; we just had to entertain them.

Our first album came out in '94. The grunge-bubble was bursting a little bit for some people. We got popular because, I guess, the times, they were a changin', as Bob Dylan said. I guess it was a shift in the currents. I'd been making my kind of music all of my life and all of a sudden it plopped me down on a moving train and I just held on for dear life. I really can't explain it. Just the right place at the right time. I guess the zeitgeist was ready to have a party and we were there to provide it.

(Kim Thayil) It was the time of our life.

(Jeff Gilbert) To be here right before it happened, right as it was happening, and right after, it was amazing. I had a ringside seat to the best show in town. The city was the show.

(Side-side note that has nothing to do with the Seattle music explosion or Almost Live!, but it's such a great story it has to be mentioned. The name of one of grunge music's more iconic albums was inadvertently inspired by a certain local clown. This is for all the people who grew up in Seattle in the '60s and '70s.)

(Kim Thayil) Our biggest album, Superunknown, that title came from the fact that Chris [Cornell] was laying on the carpet in his room, probably playing guitar, just laying on his side...he was staring at a shelf and amongst the books there were a number of VHS tapes and he had a collection of some JP Patches shows. But one of them was an episode about Superklown, and he was looking at it sideways and he thought it said Superunknown, and he was staring at this, thinking, Superunknown, that'd be a cool name for a song. That'd be a cool name for a record. And he thought, What the heck is Superunknown?—and he grabbed the VHS tape and went, "Oh, it's one of my JP Patches tapes about Superklown."

And now you know.

1992

- Rodney King riots.
- The nicotine patch is introduced.

1993

- Beanie Babies.
- Jurassic Park—The movie.
- Six people die and 167 homes are destroyed in the Puget Sound Inauguration Day storm.

1994

- Skater Nancy Kerrigan attacked.
- The Chunnel opens between England and France.
- OJ Simpson flees police in a white Ford Bronco—very slowly.
- Kurt Cobain commits suicide.

The Return of Ms. Guppy

Joe and Nancy Guppy left Almost Live! in 1989 for the bright lights of Los Angeles. They found a measure of success, no small feat as out-of-towners, but the Northwest has a powerful gravitational pull, and after three years they felt compelled to return. The manner in which they returned was not the way they expected. Nancy's return also added a new dynamic to the show: two women. For the first time in years there was a second woman on staff. It instantly gave everyone at the writer's table more options. And on top of that, the cast chemistry only improved. The vibe was electric.

(Nancy Guppy) I came home because, I will not call it a nervous breakdown, it wasn't, but I was feeling like I didn't like what we were doing down there, I didn't like our life down there. I was getting depressed. So I drove up to Seattle and I stayed with my sister. I went to therapy, it was like a mid-life crisis but I was only in my mid-thirties. So for three or four months I was really depressed. I eventually heard through the grapevine that Comedy Central was knocking on the door of Almost Live!. I had dinner with John (Keister) at the 5-Spot and told him I was interested in coming back but don't want to just do occasional bits but be on staff. He hired me. But Joe was still back in LA.

(Joe Guppy) When Nancy took the job with Almost Live! I had started to lose interest in comedy; it's hard to explain. I can't make logical sense out of it. I was just done.

(Nancy Guppy) He felt he didn't have anything more to say in that format because he'd done it for so long. I think you get to a point in your creative arc where you're done. And he was done. He'd come up for the weekends occasionally but once I was hired and doing Comedy Central and worked over the summer it became clear that Joe and I needed to be separated.

(Joe Guppy) Nancy and I separated, but not separated in the sense of divorcing but actually with the intention of getting back together. That was the plan, but at that time we couldn't take it anymore. We couldn't live together for that time. We needed a break and work on our own issues.

(Nancy Guppy) It was kind of this wild thing. I was down there visiting him one weekend and we were talking about having him come back up when we came to the realization, almost at the same time, that we can't just pick up and act like nothing has happened here, because something has happened here. So we split for, like, nine months.

(Joe Guppy) We love to tell that story because it gives a lot of hope to other couples. I think a lot of people look at a separation as a death knell. I don't know why I had the idea. Maybe it was something I picked up in therapy; I always like to read a lot of self help books and I just picked up this concept that we could do this and it would be more like a tool and hopefully rebuild the relationship. Not to say we didn't have any serious problems. I was getting ready to move back to Seattle, we were going to get an apartment together and when we got back we went, "It's not right, we're not ready." We each had this image of, like, two black spheres connected by a bar, it was just this visual image that we shared, and if that's all there was, we had this connection but everything else had to go. So when I came back to Seattle I actually moved into my parents' house and she had her place.

(Nancy Guppy) I had an apartment and this groovy job [at Almost Live!] and Joe moved in with his parents and was like, "What am I gonna do?"

(Joe Guppy) So we went to couple's counseling. And it worked.

(Nancy Guppy) We got back together and he went back to school and got his masters as a psychotherapist and I stayed with the show.

(Tracey Conway) Before Nancy returned I was the only chick for two years. I was Wendy with the Lost Boys. It was cool because I got to play everything. I got to play the tramps, I got to play the mom; you name it.

(Nancy Guppy) When I came back on the show Tracey was the deal. She was *the* woman, and she was loved and funny and I definitely felt competitive and jealous of that, but not to the extent that I was trying to undermine her.

(Bill Stainton) I had a typically naive misogynistic preconception that all women were insanely jealous of each other. So I was anticipating that I'd be spending an inordinate amount of time stopping (or at least refereeing) catfights, massaging egos, etc. I could not have been more wrong! Nancy was thrilled to have another woman on the cast to play with!

(Pat Cashman) Nancy and Tracey seemed like buddies right from the start. They shared an office. I saw nothing but friendliness from both of them for each other. I think they may have been privately glad that they had each other in an office of stinky men—and were able to collaborate on sketches reflecting a female point-of-view.

(Ed Wyatt) I think Nancy was thrilled to be back in Seattle after some hectic times in LA and Tracey was happy to have another woman around. A second woman on staff brought a wealth of opportunities, including sketches that could utilize two women as lead actors.

(Tracey Conway) I loved working with Nancy. She was so fearless. I think I'm funny but Nancy was fearless, she was just, you know unique.

(Nancy Guppy) Tracy and I together were a tremendous combination because we're so different looking and our styles are so different.

(Bill Stainton) They obviously had different looks (Tracey: tall; Nancy: short, etc.). The cool thing is that they were both so versatile that they could each play pretty much anything from a Kent hick to a Mercer Island bitch (comedy deals in stereotypes). Which meant that I now had two "utility" females (in the same way that Pat Cashman was our "utility" male — he could do anything) in my bag of tricks. They both ended up doing wonderful work together.

Tracey and Nancy playing the Bad Girls at the
Comedy Central wrap party.

Cashman being Cashman.

Facetime

Whenever you're on television it's known as facetime. Facetime is very important to on-camera talent. The more you have of it the more familiar you become to the viewer. The more familiar you become to the viewer the more ingrained you become with them. For actors, reporters, anchors and hosts, their face is part of their brand. It's simple marketing. The cast of Almost Live! had a surprisingly low level of ego—relative to what you'd normally find in the world of performing arts. At the same time, they weren't idiots. They knew that more facetime led to more recognition. They wanted their face out there and a name attached to that face. It's simple marketing. It's branding.

(Ed Wyatt) A friend of mine named Bill Jeakle, he wrote that book with me in college, had moved from Atlanta to Seattle, he was a very savvy guy. Keister was very suspicious of him because Bill was a little bit slick, Bill was a marketing guy, a sales guy, and he said, "You guys should have your names in the opening, just like they do for Saturday Night Live." Jeakle's theory was that people on the show, you knew Keister, you knew Bill Nye and after that it was the guy with the gravelly voice, that was me, the sleepy-eyed guy, that was Bob Nelson, and the woman. And he was kind of right, the rest of us really didn't have a presence and that was when we started putting our names on the open. Bill really put it in my head and so Nye and I really pushed for that because we were trying to increase our profile on the show.

(Steve Wilson) I was really insistent on doing an open that had our faces. I was the one who said, "This is what we have to do," because I was in charge of getting the open done. And when we went to Comedy Central they weren't gonna do it. I basically said, "You don't put my face in the open along with everybody else in this cast, I'm not doing it." You gotta have, like, a thirty-second open that shows the cast; the cast is what it is. I thought, You know, people will recognize us on the street, they'll see us in the streets shooting, they'll know it's us. I keep saying, "It's the magic box where people invite you into their homes, so they want to see faces."

(Nancy Guppy) Comedy is very specific. With sketch comedy, you like a particular person. You want to know who that person is. SNL does that, Kids in the Hall did it, SCTV did it. You know who they are and you want to see those people and so you have to build familiarity. You have to build those personalities. It's imperative. And that's why I thought it was so great because we all felt more acknowledged and it builds the brand like crazy.

(Bill Stainton) I don't think it's accurate to say that several cast members demanded the new open. I think the only time that really was an issue was when Joel [McHale] was made a full cast member, but wasn't in the open for an entire year. He was upset, but even then, I don't think "demanded" would be the right word.

(Joleen Winther Hughes) Almost Live! filmed one of their opening segments at the Weathered Wall.

(Bill Stainton) I can't remember what the impetus was for the Weathered Wall shoot — maybe we just thought it was time for a new open. I'm extraordinarily proud of that open — partly because, no matter what anyone says, it was my idea. We wanted to do a new open, and it occurred to me that every other sketch show open was basically a bunch of fast cuts of the various cast members. So I thought, What if we did an open with NO cuts whatsoever? Just one continuous take? I don't know who found the Weathered Wall (probably Hans-Eric Gosch), but it was perfect! We blocked the thing out, trying to put little bits in for most of the performers (e.g., Tracey playing with fire, Pat doing his pratfall, Nancy coming out of the men's room, etc.).

(Nancy Guppy) That was so fun! That was fabulous. Tracey was sitting at a table, she put her hand through a candle, Pat fell down some stairs, I came out of the men's bathroom and winked, Ed Wyatt turned around and just nodded, Wilson had a big smile and John did the stage dive. We were trying to grab a little piece of our personalities. It was really interesting and textured, and it was one long, uninterrupted shot. That was huge.

(Bill Stainton) We shot it very late at night — something like 1 or 2 am, if I remember. The actual realization and look of the open belongs almost entirely to Gary Harper, who was the photog who shot it (on film, no less!). He totally got the vision of what I wanted. We did something like 5 takes, and that was it. I still think it's the best open the show ever had: it was different, hip, and completely captured the tone of the show. I remember having to edit it when Ed Wyatt left the show. The challenge for me was, how do you edit an open that's just one continuous shot? Well, it turns out that if you do a quick (like, 5 frame) dissolve between the swish pans, it's all but imperceptible. So I was able to take Ed out and go directly from Nancy to Steve seemingly without a break. But, alas, there was no way to insert Joel into that open, so eventually we had to make the change to the black and white open (which, although it was fine, I never particularly cared for).

Photo shoot at Green Lake. And then they disinfected.

I always watch the show &
like it for the most part, but
"The Woman's Place" is not funny
or clever. I hate that.

J. Tollefsen
Sea

Constructive fan mail.

Almost Live

Bye, Bye, Bill Nye

There is an entire generation of people who only know Bill Nye from his own TV shows, Bill Nye the Science Guy or The Eyes of Nye. When Bill left Almost Live! you could reasonably argue that he became the most nationally recognizable cast member. He created a remarkably successful brand for himself. Bill loved his time on Almost Live! but he had his eyes set on bigger things.

(Steve Wilson) Bill was not part of the show after Comedy Central. He was not part of the show after '92. He was shooting the Bill Nye the Science Guy shows while we were shooting that summer. He would shoot his show and come over and appear here and there. But after that he was done with the thing.

(Bill Stainton) There were a few times where Bill would say, "No I can't really do that because the Science Guy wouldn't do that. I've got a reputation now." And what was happening was that it became clear to me that Bill's future wasn't with Almost Live!, this Science Guy thing was going to be big.

(Bill Nye) I do remember the first conversation being with John Keister. He said to me, in so many words, "You've got to decide what you want to do, Almost Live! or The Science Guy." The bit that brought it into focus for me was written by Ed Wyatt. It was contemporary with the Nike "Bo Knows" campaign. Bo Jackson knows baseball. Bo knows football, etc... It was "Bill knows basketball; Bill knows bicycles; Bill knows weather?" which went well. Along about that time was the Reebok campaign for cross-training shoes. Ed's bit was about cross training and cross-dressing. I played basketball in high-heels. It was funny. But then, I knew I had to choose. Could I cross lines like that for comedy, and then be a kids' show host? Probably not. Comedy or science education?

(Steve Wilson) Bill Stainton was the one who said, "We really need you on full time." As far as I know Bill Nye wanted to stay on as a staff member but he didn't want to work 40 hours a week because he had his own show.

(Bill Nye) The second conversation that I remember was with Jim Sharp in the summer, when Comedy Central contracted for a big bloc of the shows. Jim said, "Seems like you've been avoiding us." I had been, a little. I was at a crossroads.

(Bill Stainton) I had to have a heart to heart talk with him and say, "Bill, I think we're holding you back. As long as you're on Almost Live! you can't fully be Bill Nye the Science Guy." So I let him go. And I thought it was a very amicable meeting, until I read about it in the paper. Somebody interviewed him about it and the interview said, "Yea, Stainton fired me. I didn't see it coming." I mean, there were only two people in the room—me and Bill Nye, and I recollected going, "Oh, well that went better than I thought." But it was tough because Nye was becoming this breakout star; I had to fire my breakout star because it was no longer a fit.

(Bill Nye) The conversation with Bill Stainton was indeed amicable and a relief, leastways as I remember it. I really don't remember the newspaper saying I was bitter. Did a reporter take the time to ask me about Almost Live!? Or did someone in the building comment on some frustrated remark I made? Hmm… At any rate, negotiations for salary at Almost Live! were always troublesome and a concern of mine. I was making much less than I could as a professional engineer. I was supporting my comedy habit with part time engineering contract jobs. We all can suppress memories.

(Scott Schaefer) I got to know some people at Fox. How it works in Hollywood is you get to know people on a show and if the show gets canceled you commiserate with them and they eventually get a gig on another show and they'll say, "Hey you should try to get a gig on the show," so it becomes a nomadic lifestyle moving from show to show. I think the longest I worked on a show was two years on America's Funniest People, then I worked on the Arsenio Hall show, then I sold a couple of pilots to CBS. Then around '93 or '94 Bill Nye called and he said he needed a senior writer to work on [his] show. So my wife and I at the time, we're having trouble buying a house in LA, we couldn't afford a house while at the same time this is what we went through, and this was a real turning point, we went through fires, floods, earthquakes and the Rodney King riots. So that was the four Horsemen of the Apocalypse of Los Angeles for us. So when Bill Nye offered us the job I was thinking, This is a crazy town. So we move back to Seattle and I worked on Bill Nye the Science Guy and won three national Emmy's and I've been back ever since.

Oh yea, I remember that sketch!

- **A Woman's Place**
  Tracey Conway and Hollyce Phillips in :30 teases promoting their next show, with topics like, How to make your bangs go a foot straight up in the air—Dealing with husbands who insist on wearing their tool belts to bed—And women and guilt: Why it's better just to tell him to go burn in hell.

- **Married with Badges**
  John Keister and Tracey Conway are cops whose marriage issues keep surfacing on the job.

- **East Side Story**
  Bellevue, Kirkland, et al get the musical treatment. Sing along now! We are the trash of Fac-to-ri-a, our colors clash in Fac-to-ri-a, grow a mustache in Fac-to-ri-a, we all get smashed in Fac-to-ri-a.

- **Uncle Fran's Musical Forest**
  Hey boys and girls! Bob Nelson plays the inappropriate singing kids show host who clearly doesn't understand the concept of being a kids show host. Mr. Raccoon will have to agree.

- **Seattle Summer**
  Where everyone makes a beeline to Green Lake for that first exposure to blindingly white winter skin.
  And then it's over.

Comedy Central

Once upon a time Almost Live! was on Comedy Central for two years. Yes, two years. Whenever I tell people that they look utterly surprised. The truly surprising part about the story though is how long it took the cast and crew to tape enough material to fill that two-year commitment.

(John Keister) After the show started doing as well as it did I thought we could probably take this nationally.

(Bill Stainton) Comedy Central was this fledgling network and was really looking for programming and we had this ready-made show. We had a studio; we had a huge backlog of material.

(John Keister) I had a lot of contacts in Los Angeles and one of them was Jim Sharp who was still down there after he left Almost Live! with Ross. So I talked to Jim and I said, "Look, we've got a lot of material," and he said, "Send me a sample," and he got together with some people he knew down there and within just this short amount of time, we were in all these big meetings, a deal was put together.

(Ross Shafer) I guess we were naïve or young or didn't know what we were doing because we never did trademark the name Almost Live! and we should have. Because what Jim Sharp found out when he took it to Comedy Central was that, hey, you guys don't own this name. And a comedian I knew named Jeff Valdez in Phoenix trademarked the name and Comedy Central had to pay

Jeff I think about 35 thousand dollars just for that name. It was probably not a pleasant conversation they had at Comedy Central.

(Jim Sharp) I had a guy I was doing television with, he was a line producer in LA and his wife had a connection to a company called Worldvision which was a syndicator, and we put together this tape of comedy from Almost Live! and we took out the local stuff that might not play well and it got viewed by Comedy Central and they ordered I think sixty shows. We bought from KING what we thought were the "A" bits and then we created a lot of new stuff.

(John Keister) I mean we had a lot of stuff in the can but yeah, we were writing a lot of stuff. By that time, Bob had joined the show, Ed had joined the show and Nancy didn't like Los Angeles and she came back and so she came back to the show and Tracy had been on the show for a while.

(Bob Nelson) Comedy Central wasn't the Comedy Central it is today, but still, it was great.

(Jim Sharp) We created sixty shows over two and a half months. It was crazy, we went up and every two weeks we would shoot sixteen shows. We pretty much killed ourselves.

(Steve Wilson) It almost killed me. But I knew going into it that it was going to be 16 weeks. Sixteen weeks of non-stop. With regular Almost Live! we worked all week to do one show. With the 16 week thing we started doing one show in the morning and one show in the afternoon, then we increased that to doing two shows in the morning and three shows in the afternoon/evening. It was incredible. At our peak I think we did about ten shows in one weekend.

(Bill Stainton) And we did that all summer long. It was the summer from hell. Oh my god, it was brutal.

(Tracey Conway) Oh, it was insane, great insane but Wilson in particular, I don't know if he ever took a day off.

(Steve Wilson) It was the hardest work I'd ever done in my life but it was well worth it.

(John Keister) Being on Comedy Central for a few years, every day on Comedy Central for a few years and people on the show were able to make a lot of money during those years. It's not like it made up for everything but there was pretty big cash in there. Bob Nelson, who had never been anyplace in his life on vacation, other than the Oregon coast, was able to travel through Britain with his wife, which had been a boyhood dream of his, as a result of the money from Comedy Central.

(Bob Nelson) It was fun and we were all young enough to burn the candle and pull it off.

(Pat Cashman) I will tell you, I have copies of all those Comedy Central shows and I have looked at them and said, "I have actually no memory of doing that. I know that's me standing there and doing that but I cannot remember anything about it." It's just amazing that you can't remember something, not a goddamn thing. And it's like we were sleepwalking through that, because I was doing early morning radio on top of it. What a great opportunity, but, man, was it difficult to do.

(Bill Stainton) My personal opinion is that once we finished that and we went back to our regular show at the end of the summer, we never really had the same spark. We went on for another six or seven years—I think season eight was our pinnacle of creativity—and then we did the Comedy Central shows and I think it just drained us. My own personal opinion is that after Comedy Central we just coasted through season nine, just because we were beat, and then we never quite got the same spark. The show was still good but the energy just felt different.

The cast and crew for Almost Live! on Comedy Central.
It took a lot of bodies.

1995

- Oklahoma City bombing.
- OJ Simpson found innocent of murder.
- DVDs debut.
- Four firefighters die in the Pang warehouse fire.

1996

- Sound Transit is approved by voters. Commuter trains and light-rail lines planned.
- Charles and Diana divorce.

Dying is Easy, Comedy is Hard

Eons ago, while character actor Edmund Gwenn lay ill in bed, director and screenwriter George Seaton swung by for a visit. Seaton said to Gwenn, "This must be terribly difficult for you." Gwenn supposedly replied, "Not nearly as difficult as playing comedy." That eventually became the well-known theater trope, Dying is easy; comedy is hard. To find out if there's any truth to it just ask Tracey Conway. On January 21st, 1995, seconds after wrapping an episode of Almost Live! Tracey collapsed on stage and died. Being dead and everything Tracey has no memory of any of it. What she knows is what people tell her happened. Based on those last two sentences you can see that she somehow survived. Here's how it played out.

(Bill Stainton) We'd just finished taping the show. You know how at the end of SNL when all the cast members wave, the music plays and the credits roll? Well we did the same thing. Mostly it's just a timing device, because the show has to come in at a certain time, to the second, every week, and we can stay on this shot as long as we need. So we do that, the show fades to black and we stay there and chat with the audience while Steve, up in the booth, checks the tape to make sure the show stuck to the tape.

(Bob Nelson) I was standing right next to Tracey and she sort of leaned over towards me and said, "I don't feel so…" and then she just dropped.

(Steve Wilson) By the time I'd taken the headset off and gone down to the studio—it takes me about ten seconds to get down there—she'd already hit the floor.

(Bill Stainton) One of the earlier sketches we'd done in the show was a taped piece called ERR, it was a take off on the TV show ER about a bumbling hospital staff.

(Pat Cashman) [When Tracey collapsed] I think the audience started laughing because they thought it was a callback to the ERR bit from earlier in the show.

(Hans-Eric Gosch) I don't think any of us at first thought what was happening was what was actually happening. We thought Tracey was being funny, because she was.

(Nancy Guppy) I saw her out of the corner of my eye start to collapse and I'm thinking, Oh for god sakes, how much attention do you need? I seriously thought that. I thought she was doing some goofy thing. And then it's, wait a minute, she's on the ground doing these very strange physical moves.

(Bill Stainton) Her eyes were rolled back in her head and she's making a gurgling sound that did not sound human.

(Tracey Conway) The actual name is ventricular fibrillation. It's not a heart attack, it's a problem with your electrical system; it's a short circuit that causes [your heart] to beat erratically, chaotically. I was without my own heartbeat for almost 20 minutes. I was clinically dead. There's a difference between clinically and biologically dead. You cannot come back from biologically dead. On the incident report, question 24, it says, patient condition on arrival of fire department unit, and there are only two options to that question, alive or dead, and dead was the little circle filled in.

(Bob Nelson) I'm sure it was just a few minutes for the ambulance to get there but it seemed like forever. It was pretty grim when she was on the floor. It was pretty terrifying. By the time that happened we were like family.

(Bill Stainton) I would love to say I leapt in to action and took control; I didn't really. I think it was John that said to the audience, you don't want to say, "Is there a doctor in the house?" because that sounds like a joke on a joke, so he asks if anyone has any medical training. And there were these two volunteer firemen who knew CPR. So they're doing CPR and I run upstairs rummaging through Tracey's stuff. I knew that she had a heart condition and it ran in her family and she was on medication and someone will want to know what that medication is, and I also called her family, which was tough, because as far as I knew she might be dead by now. It certainly didn't look good. So while the firemen are pumping Tracey I remember running out, I think with Keister, to wait for the EMTs. And it's amazing when you read the report of how quickly they got there, it seemed like it took them a half an hour, it was like, "Where the F are they? God dammit, where are they?" If you'd asked me in that moment I would have said it's been twenty minutes, and I think they got there in like three minutes or something like that. Maybe seven.

(Steve Wilson) I run outside, we can hear sirens but they're not close enough, and John and I are out there, "Where the hell are they? When are they gonna get here?" So we literally run out to Dexter Avenue and stand in the middle of Dexter, I'm looking north and John's looking south, and finally we see it. We're waving our arms, "This way, this way, in there, in there!" They drive in and park inside the prop room.

(Nancy Guppy) When the medics came in I remember thinking, Walk faster! Why are you walking? Run!

(Steve Wilson) They bring the paddles out and, boom; I think they zapped her, like six times, and we're all standing there, "Come on, come on Tracey." Finally they got a pulse and took her away. So we're all, like, we're going to Harborview and everybody took off in their cars. So I'm there in the studio by myself and there's rubber tubes and stuff all over the floor. So I cleaned it up, picked up all the needles and tubes and mopped the floor, because I didn't want [people seeing] any blood on that floor.

(Bill Stainton) So they took her and we all drove up to Harborview and we're in this little waiting room and it was really weird because the entire Almost Live! cast is there and there's a TV in the room and we're watching Almost Live!, because by this time it's 11:30. So we're watching ERR, and it was a good show, it was a really good show and we're thinking, Do we laugh? As far as we know Tracey is 40 feet away from us in another room, dead or dying.

(Pat Cashman) I remember some people were actually watching it and I said, "I don't want to watch this," and then the doctor comes in and says, "I think she's going to probably pull through but she's probably going to go through some psychological trauma from it."

(Nancy Guppy) When she woke up she had no short-term memory. At all. She had no sense of what had happened.

(Steve Wilson) The next day going to visit her she was doing what's called cycling, where she'd be like, "Steve! What are you doing here? What am I doing here? How did I get here?" "Well you had an accident." "Oh. How long have I been here?" "Overnight." "Oh." Then someone else would walk in and it would be, "Bob! What are you doing here? What am I doing here?"

(Tracey Conway) I don't remember anything of the day I collapsed. Everything I know is from what people told me.

(Bill Stainton) She'll tell you the odds of her surviving—she's done the medical research—for every minute your brain goes without oxygen your chances of surviving go down ten percent and she was down for like 13 or 14 minutes, so you do the math, she shouldn't be alive. Somehow she really lucked out.

(Tracey Conway) My first memory is being in the ambulance from Harborview to UW where they implanted my defibrillator. But before that I'm told I was conscious and talking. A lot. People always want to know, "Did you see the light? What happened?" But I don't remember anything. But my nurses, my friend who was there and even my family, those first days when I was at

Harborview I kept saying the same things over and over, "Where's the hall? Why didn't you leave me in that hall? I was in that white hall, why didn't you leave me in that white hall? Where's Mark? I was with Mark, where's Mark? We were in the hall!" Well, Mark's my older brother who also died of cardiac arrest, six years before I did. Now I don't remember any of this, none of it, but people tell me that's all I would say for days. I actually find that really comforting because I'm not making it up, it's what sane people said I said.

(Bill Stainton) We had the next week off, so two weeks later we're back on the air and Tracey was on the show.

(Pat Cashman) Like nothing had ever happened.

(Bill Stainton) She F-ing died and didn't miss a show.

How Do They Come Up With This Stuff?

In one of Bill Watterson's icon Calvin and Hobbes comic strips Hobbes asks Calvin if he has an idea for a story yet. Calvin replies that he's waiting for inspiration. He says you can't turn on creativity like a faucet. You have to be in the right mood. That right mood, as Calvin points out, is, of course, last-minute panic. The cast of Almost Live!, however, *did* have to turn their creativity on like a faucet. The TV beast needed feeding every week. The show didn't have to be perfect it had to be done. So how did it get done, and what were some of their more memorable sketches?

(Bill Nye) We showed up Tuesdays with ideas for bits and full scripts for bits for the following Saturday. We all had ideas. Good ones came from Joe, Ed, and Bill Stainton. Great ones came from Pat. Then there was Bob Nelson — Wow!

(Tracey Conway) It is a comedy show and in these pitch meetings you say a lot of things that will never go on the air. We could have all been hauled into HR many a time. When I first started I was the only woman on the staff and my very first meeting with the guys I was very nervous. I had a friend who said, "Why don't you bring something to help break the ice?" And she gave me this thing that she thought would be funny if I put on the table before I read my first few ideas. And so I did. It was a little wind-up, hopping penis. She said, "Just say everyone else in the room has one of these so I figured I should to."

(Bill Stainton) There were three kinds of sketches that got pitched: There are the ones that you know are just a shoe in; they're so freakishly good. You can't wait to put this on the air. Then there are the ones that are so bad, you know, "This just sucks, there's no way this is going on the air." Most of them were in that middle range, "Yea, that could work, I could see that working." A lot of mine were in that range.

(Ed Wyatt) It was John's show but I think Bill Stainton, the producer, had final call on sketches. If anything crossed the line Bill had that sense and working with the sales department, stuff that John didn't really understand. Bill had all the relationships.

(Bob Nelson) I think Almost Live! was unusual for most sketch shows. You hear all these stories, particularly about Saturday Night Live, but everyone at Almost Live! was very supportive. I think in my first few pitch meetings it was very nerve-wracking and it took me a while to get the rhythm to finally get some sketches on, after that it was a matter of all of these people were becoming friends and you started taking chances.

(Nancy Guppy) There wasn't a crazy amount of ego; there was a lot of freedom. I'd heard the stories about SNL. Nightmare! I would have died in that situation, it would have murdered me, no way I could have handled that crucible. But with Almost Live!, look, people wanted their stuff on the air, you really wanted your stuff in, you wanted the exposure, you wanted to be seen and be funny. But it wasn't brutal. I fought for stuff all the time. I'd be like, "I can't believe this piece isn't getting the green light!" Sometimes I was right, sometimes I was wrong. Bill and John set the tone of a level playing field.

(Bill Stainton) Nancy used to drive me crazy because as a producer I would sometime turn down a sketch of hers and she would fight for it. I mean she would come into my office, and I'm like, "Oh boy, here we go again."

(Hans-Eric Gosch) If you wrote and successfully pitched a sketch at the table meeting it was understood that it was also your opportunity (and responsibility) to direct the shoot, as well as work closely in the editing room with Ralph Bevins, the show's videographer. Ralph's contribution to Almost Live! was immense. As the sole photographer/editor for all taped sketches his fingerprints and choices are all over Almost Live!. The sole exception being Pat Cashman's work. Pat owned his sketches to the very end because he was also a genius in the editing booth. Crazy talented.

(Steve Wilson) Pat was bullet proof. He was the Phil Hartman of Almost Live!. Most of the time he worked solo and he would just present the tape and we'd be like, "This is amazing." Pat really never needed to pitch. If you look at the stuff he did on the show it was really good stuff. He was probably one of the best comedic actors we had on the show.

(Ralph Bevins) Pat Cashman was a supremely talented person. I don't think other people were jealous of that; they were just entertained and excited to hear his ideas. He was kind of the go-to guy. They'd say, "Hey Pat, we need a funny open," and he'd be like, "Okay."

(John Keister) Pat would always come up with some great bit for the show but a lot of times he would come in toward the end of the meeting because he was working on radio.

(Pat Cashman) Well, my schedule didn't really line up. I was doing radio. I think writers meetings started around 10:00 and I'd been on the air till then, so I would arrive later at the table. Between you and me, I hated to go. I thought it worked out great for me because I hated writers meetings. It was like going to an audition, you've got to read your stuff in front of everybody else. What if they don't laugh? What if they don't get it? It's just painful, because in your own head, "I know this is a good idea, I know I can pull this off. Why do I have to sell it to the room?" So whenever I could avoid that I did.

(Ed Wyatt) Bill Stainton was an awkward one because he was the producer, so if he green lighted his piece, naturally if it wasn't great, if we didn't think it was worthy of it you couldn't say anything. But that said, most of Bill's stuff was good but occasionally one would slip through and you'd think, "Hmmmm, who's going to tell him that really doesn't quite work?" John was the only one who could say, "Eh, I don't really like that piece."

(Bill Stainton) I think I was harder on myself than anyone else. There were ideas that I pitched that had somebody else pitched them they probably would have gotten on the show. I think in fifteen years I had only one or two that were really, really good. So I was usually in that middle range, and since I was the deciding vote I tended to vote against myself because I didn't want it to look like favoritism. There was only one time where I really pushed mine. Every Christmas we would do Christmas carols, but re-written for Seattle. There was one I did for Carol of the Bells for when the Mariners were threatening to leave if we didn't build a retractable dome. So mine was like…"We need a dome/build us a dome/If there's no dome, we're leaving home/We want it now/We need it now/Pay for it now/We don't care how/We need a place to play on a sunny day when the freaking roof rolls away/Just be certain that the plans are pleasin' if you want to have another season." I just thought that was brilliant. I really, really loved it. But somebody else pitched lyrics something like, "We're being screwed/We're being screwed." Everything was screwed, and the rest of the table really liked that, but I said, "No, no, mine's too smart, we're going with mine. Dammit, we're going with that one." That was the only time I really put my foot down.

(Ed Wyatt) It was competitive, everyone wanted their stuff on the show but I think I can honestly say that everyone there was a nice person at heart, I don't think there was ever any knockdown, drag-out fights.

(John Keister) For show business, it's extremely strange. I have never had a situation like that, where everybody was like, everybody got along so well. And it's not just a Seattle thing, because I have been involved in things in Seattle where there are big, knockdown, drag-out fights and I have worked on shows that have not been very good, this one was both a good show and people got along. If there was tension the tension came from that we didn't have access to enough equipment and we were always being asked to do more with less, which I thought was really bizarre because even though we were winning all these awards…

(Bill Stainton) The show won over 100 Emmys.

(John Keister) …we were the number one show and yet we were always getting squeezed, we were always getting squeezed for stuff. When we would win awards Comedy Central would send us like a bouquet, they would send us like, "Hey, we see you won the IRIS Award again," and there would be big presents and stuff. People at KING would be like, as if it was kind of – it was like being on the Russian hockey team, it's like if the Seahawks win two Super Bowls in a row, "Yeah, whatever." There was this expectation that we didn't need anything, that we could do all this stuff.

(Ed Wyatt) There usually wasn't a lot of collaboration on the creative. There was if you specifically asked someone for help. Something like High-Five'n White Guys is a collaborative thing. Bill Nye and I had this idea because we'd go to Mariners games; we had season tickets. We'd see all these people high-five'n and we started joking about guys who high-five'd over everything. That became the High-Five'n White Guys.

(Steve Wilson) The first one was simply us just running around high-fiving. No real jokes, other than people on the street gushing about how cool we were. It was a pretty quick throwaway. But it got such a strong reaction, so we made it a returning piece. We made up scenarios as we walked around…or as we met interesting characters. There was never really anything written down on paper, we just went out, picked a place, started shooting, had lunch, shot some more. It was all fixed in the edit. The "White Guys" changed over the years when people left the show. I however, never left so I am in every one of them, which, I guess, makes me the whitest High-Five'n White guy there is. It is the only bit people still stop me in supermarkets for. They want a high-five.

(Mike Boydstun) For the High-Five'n White Guys we never had permits. We had places that we shot at a lot. We had the Almost Live! alley; this alley near KING 5 where we would frequently shoot; we shot in a lot of the  same places. [Our crew] really wasn't that big, it was just me, an intern maybe, and whoever was on camera.

(Steve Wilson) We never got permits. If we were gonna shoot at Seattle Center or, as we found out, The Pike Place Market, we were challenged for permits. But by the time they found us or sent someone out, we were done. I do remember the shoot at the Pike Place Market (not a White Guys shoot) where we were shooting on the sidewalk, and the security guards said that it was private property and we couldn't shoot. So we move out in the middle of the street and shot. Public property there.

(John Keister) There was a bit that Pat and I did with Dave Kreig. He had been invited to the Pro Bowl the year before but John Elway was selected in favor of him that year. We did this bit where we were kind of giving him lot of crap about it. He was at this party and we were watching the Pro Bowl with him and it was like, "Boy, did you see how well Elway threw that ball to – I mean just right on the numbers!" And he was getting angrier and angrier and angrier.

(Bill Stainton) Cashman would say, "Were you that one who threw that famous pass to Largent?" And Krieg's like, "Yea, yea, that was me." Cashman says, "I don't know how he caught that, it was way over his head." Basically we were making fun of his ability as a quarterback and he was willing to play along.

(Hans-Eric Gosch) Because we were shooting most days, scouting and negotiating the locations we needed for tape pieces could be a ton of work. One week you were borrowing a sports car to parody a new James Bond film, shutting down a mortuary for four hours to tape a funeral sketch or begging to shoot in a hospital operating room for half a day. Of course, we never had money to pay the businesses we borrowed things from so you saw a lot of *promotional consideration provided by* messages and personal thank yous in the end credits each week. Special seating at live tapings was reserved each week, too, for friends and businesses that helped us pull the show together.

JOKES -- SHOW 923

Ron Reagan Jr. was in town to interview Emmett Watson. Reagan Jr. said the interview was great, because he found the only man in the world ~~who~~ less coherent than his father.

There is a new 800 number for people who think Hanford's radioactivity made them sick. There's also a 900 number for those who think the radioactivity made them horny.

The United States government is considering naming the Lynx an endangered species. It would join the Bobcat, the Pinto, and the Dodge Dart.

Spokane County's burning season is officially over. That means no more improvements for awhile to downtown Spokane.

A poster titled "Slam and Jam" features the Sonics' Shawn Kemp, and Jeff Ament from Pearl Jam. There is a similar poster featuring Nirvana's Kurt Cobain and ex-Seahawk Kelly Stouffer called "Wired and Fired."

Naturalist comic strip hero Mark Trail will soon be getting married. The announcement comes after an out-of-wedlock child with Cathy.

For the first time ever, the Queen of England has opened Buckingham Palace to the public. The first visitors were three Irish guys dressed in black and carrying unmarked packages.

The state government is considering a tax on sports and entertainment tickets. Although Mariners and Sonics tickets would be taxed, Seahawks games would not, since they don't qualify as entertainment or sports.

A bank has seized the assets of the Nutri-System diet center, causing a number of them to close. When asked why, the bank said that the company president and CEO failed to make their goal weights.

The Dalai Lama's summer visit to Seattle has been postponed. A spokesperson for the Tibetan holy man says he wants to come back when the Mariners are in the middle of a homestand.

The town of Sultan is using country music "line dancing" as a way to relieve pressure and increase community spirit. In Kent, they're doing the same thing with "The Hustle."

(Ed Wyatt) I did a lot of my writing at the Romper Room, it's now called Tini Bigs, my friend Keith owned it and I'd go there and just sit in the corner and write and have a couple of drinks. They really took care of me, they'd slip me a couple of drinks, I'd pay for plenty but they also gave me plenty. I'd write some stuff there and then I'd take it in. We'd have a meeting on Tuesdays and we'd bring our ideas in. You might read a whole sketch or just suggest making fun of, say, that new commercial, and then people could add to it. You'd look at the week and go, okay it's a half hour, so we'd start with a cold open, that little bit at the start of the show where it would say, (show name) will not be seen tonight. One of mine was Tonya Harding's dance party will not be seen tonight, where you see a bunch of people dancing and then some guy came out and starts whacking them with a stick and they all fall down.

(Steve Wilson) We figured out a template that we stuck with. Cold open, open, monologue, a taped bit—the best taped bit, the really good ones we front-loaded. Go to break, come back out, studio bit, whether it's an apartment sketch or a game show. Go to break, third act, maybe a little teeny bit goes here, then the Late Report or the John Report. Go to break, come back, little teeny bit and good-bye.

(Ed Wyatt) So you'd fill in the holes with what you need, so you'd say, "Okay, Bob's got this piece here, that'll work in segment three, let's do that this week." So you'd have to figure out the taped pieces first because they had to be edited. The live stuff you'd add later. John's opening monologue you might not figure out until Friday or even Saturday because you want it to be contemporary, topical.

(Tracey Conway) I remember [Nancy] pitched to me a sketch when we were doing Comedy Central and she was living in an apartment up on Capitol Hill and she got stuck in traffic. I think she was driving into work and just had this song in her head.

(Nancy Guppy) I wrote the sketch "Me" because I was driving to work one day—this is the thing about pulling from real life—I was late and I was pissed off because people were going too slow in front of me, even though they were actually going the speed limit, it's just that I was late and so I was in a rage. I caught myself and started laughing and started singing some tune and added words and thought it was kind of funny. It was, "Everyone's getting on my nerves/ Everyone's stupider than me/Why won't you do the things I do/I'm right and you're wrong/Me!" So there was the bit,

so I wrote it up and pitched it. We did a couple of them with cast members playing different people and then the best one was when Dave Grohl came on, and he was so good! And of course, I broke his Tom Petty guitar.

(Bill Nye) I have watched Roscoe's Rug Emporium perhaps a hundred times. I laugh out loud just thinking about What Stupid Thing Will Dale Ellis Do Next?

(Ed Wyatt) Cashman's Roscoe's Rug Emporium. Absolutely brilliant.

(Joel McHale) Oh yea. Incredible. Incredible. Pat was so good and so funny. The man was like Rumplestiltskin; comedy just came out of him. He would just manufacture it from the air.

(Steve Wilson) For Roscoe's Rug Emporium Pat explained it to me and I said, "You should just do this live." When I say live, I mean live on tape. We did two takes of it. The take that we used was take number one. We sort of roughly read through it once and the only direction I gave him was start slow and when you get to these words—and I put asterisk in the teleprompter—bump it up a little bit. So you go from one to two to three to four, by the time you get to the end of the bit you're at ten. So he went from one to two to about seven. So when he got to the end of the bit he had to go to twelve. He's truly, honest to god, almost passing out when he gets to the very end of that thing. He's screaming so loud he can't catch his breath. When he was in the middle of it I'm thinking, Oh my god, he's still got two more pages of copy and he's screaming. It's the best performance on Almost Live! ever.

(Pat Cashman) The next day there was a note, and I suspect it was from Ross, and it said that was the longest, loudest laughter that we've ever had on this show. I thought that's pretty cool.

(Ed Wyatt) I think Billy Quan was groundbreaking.

(Darrell Suto) So we're out taking a long lunch, and John says, "I've got this idea for a generic action movie. It's a movie trailer for movie that's just the best parts." So it had a Rambo scene with a gun, then a James  Bond thing where there's an ejector seat in the car and all it is is just one scene after another where we would recreate a generic action movie. Just the good parts. And so one of them was, "Let's do Bruce Lee." And what we did wasn't even so much a Bruce Lee thing but a slap-sticky thing where he punches the guy and he flies through the air.

(John Keister) The Generic Action Movie sketch wasn't a great bit but we liked the ninja part. We started throwing around ideas on how we could do something with it. Then I came up with this idea, "What if the guy was like a Miss Manners-type person who would get really upset over small breaches in etiquette?" Our photographers were like frustrated filmmakers and we were really fascinated at the time with the stuff that was coming out of Hong Kong—the films of Chow-Yun Fat and John Woo; films that hadn't yet gained a lot of attention in the United States. I would submit that we were the first that were doing these Kung fu parodies. I saw that segment ripped off in a lot of commercials and movies. Mike Myers in Wayne's World 2 clearly ripped off Billy Quan. Mike Myers told me he really enjoyed watching Almost Live!. Jim Sharp's girlfriend, Courtney, was a make up artist on

Saturday Night Live and we would go back there—I also knew a few people that wrote for Saturday Night Live—and we would be able to go back stage and Courtney would say, "Oh, Mike wanted me to tell you how much he liked, you know, this scene and that scene." Then I watched Wayne's World 2 and I thought, Yea, he really does like it.

(Darrell Suto) I think the first Billy Quan was Enter the Diner where the bad guy didn't leave a tip and it hurts the waitress's feelings and of course the fight ensues and Keister's dispatched.

(John Keister) We picked Darrell Suto to play Billy, he was one of our camera operators and a friend and Asian, and we said, "Hey, why don't you try it?" At first it was just a small part in that Generic Action Movie bit and then he became a regular character. We even had publicity photos of him made because so many people liked that segment. We even sold Billy Quan tee shirts. We sold about 500 in a real short time. He was really one of the most popular characters.

(Darrell Suto) I was never that comfortable doing it. It wasn't really my thing to be in front of the camera. But just like anything else you just learn to do it. I even tried to do the voice myself but I wasn't very good at it. But of course, Pat Cashman just put it over the top. Everyone tried the voice. We really didn't know quite what voice to do. John tried the voice, Steve Wilson tried, Mike Boydstun gave it a try. If you go back and look at some old ones you can see we were just experimenting with it. We didn't even know what the lines were; we just did the action. It would be like, "Just keep shaking your fist and we'll figure out the dialogue later."

(Mike Boydstun) To get the effect of Billy flying through the air when he would leap to kick someone, we had a pair of foam legs and some black drawstring pants. I would cradle the camera around my waist area and hold the legs up  in front. It wasn't easy running around like that.

(Darrell Suto) Here's the weirdest thing, it was just a bit on the show; it was the same thing every time. The script changes were maybe just different props. There'd be an insult, some defiant reaction, then there's a fight. Then at the end the bad guy loses. If you look at them one after another it's just a template.

One time we threw a dummy off the building. Well, KING is all windows, like a big ant farm, so when the dummy fell by somebody saw it and completely flipped out. They thought somebody had fallen off the roof.

(John Keister) That segment won a lot of awards. It actually won some pretty prestigious awards for editing and stuff. It won the International Monitor Award for editing. The awards were actually handed out at Carnegie Hall. Evening Magazine had a story up for a Monitor Award and they didn't win but Billy Quan did win. It was such typical KING stuff, they wouldn't send anybody from Almost Live! to an awards ceremony but would, of course, send the Evening people. And they ended up collecting our award for us.

(Nancy Guppy) I loved Jet Guy. It's a completely idiotic bit. I love guys falling off buildings.

(Ralph Bevins) Jet Guy was my idea. It was based on this character named Commando Cody that was in Republic movie serials in the '50s, and so I loved that. And I guess I always thought there was something funny about the flying gear—that his only control that you could see was an up and down switch. It just didn't make sense to me. Bill Nye actually helped me formulate the idea. The character's name was Guy Morris, Jet Guy; I

mean it was so stupid. And he helped me do the costume and the helmet, which was just cardboard. The whole thing was cheesy, which was great. His weapons in his war against crime looked crappy, which was great. So when I broached the idea people liked it but I was sure it was going to be taken away from me and Pat would play Jet Guy, but Pat or someone said, "Why don't you do it?" I was like, "I can't act, I have no acting experience; I'm horrible." But they said, "Go for it," and I'm kind of glad that they did because I really thought it would be cool to be Jet Guy. It was the same script every time with the same dialogue with the professor saying, "I've got a new weapon in your war against crime." "Great, what is it?" "This!" And then I screw it up and die. Bill Nye really was into it, he really liked being the professor but he was busy for some reason so Bill Stainton had the idea of getting Russell Johnson, the Professor from Gilligan's Island. That was awesome.

(Bill Nye) I remember frequent references to Bob's brilliant "The Ineffectual Middle Management Suckups." Comments like, "Have you guys been eavesdropping on our meetings?" were common from strangers.

(Jeff Renner) I think they had one skit where somebody brought a python or a boa constrictor in and the snake got loose or else they went to find it after the skit was done and they thought they'd put it away and it wasn't where it was supposed to be, and they never did find that.

(Tracey Conway) This was a very funny sketch called, well we called it "Box of Snakes," but I think the sketch was called "The New Boss."

(John Keister) The idea came when we were sitting around the office and we were wondering why it was necessary to hire increasingly mean News Directors. Then I said, "Pretty soon they'll start looking outside the human species for candidates. Like the new boss is...a box of snakes."

(Tracey Conway) The idea was there was this horrible boss who was bad, but then he ends up leaving and we're all so relieved because there's a new boss. But then someone comes running up and says, "Oh my god, you know who the new boss is? A box of snakes!"

(John Keister) But it's mumbled so it's not quite clear what they said.

(Tracey Conway) "Who? What?" "A box of snakes!" "What?" "The new boss is a Box of Snakes!"—and then you cut to this office where we're all looking into this glass [box] and sure enough it was this box just writhing with real snakes. So we had to hire someone to bring in all these snakes.

(John Keister) I think it was Bill Stainton who knew—what is it called—a herpetologist? Someone who studies snakes? Anyway, this guy brings in all these boas and we do the bit. "Jim, the boss wants to see you." Someone would walk into the office and you'd hear screams. Afterwards the people come to pick up the snakes and they're, like, "We brought 12 snakes and now there's only 11." And we're, like, "That's impossible, we never touched them."

(Tracey Conway) The lore here is, and I honestly don't know if this is true or just a story, that one of them crawled off and disappeared somewhere and lives at [our old studios] to this day on the mice in some of the air ducts.

(John Keister) All I know is that to cover our bases we had to put out a memo around the station letting everyone know that there was a possibility a snake escaped.

(Jeff Renner) I would say, while giving tours, "Do watch out, we have a security snake on patrol here." Some people thought it was pretty funny, but others looked distinctly uncomfortable.

(Joel McHale) One sketch I really liked was called Hey Lenny! It was a sketch that I think Bob wrote for Pat and me where we played these dumb thugs. He was the classy thug and I was the idiot and we would do nice things to people, like, we would throw them against the walls and then we'd give them five dollars to go buy something nice for their wife or girlfriend, but we would scare the hell out of them the whole time. That was near and dear to my heart.

(Tracey Conway) John wrote [Worst girlfriend in the world] for me based on some of his own girlfriends and a friend of his, a very close friend of his. She was so much fun to play, but I'm so much not like her that I would do a take and he'd say, "Okay that's great,"  you know, he was very gentle with me, "So, okay, but push it, you know, you're being, you're too nice, you have to just be cold, super cold." It was really fun to play her.

(Ed Wyatt) Bob's Uncle Fran's stuff was great. Uncle Fran's Musical Forest where it's a kids' show with a host who doesn't want to do a kids' show; that was brilliant.

For the first time in history, Boeing engineers and technical employees went on a one-day strike Tuesday. They said it felt strange to strike because walking the picket line required standing up on the job.

Canadian tourists are furious at a Florida newspaper, which called them "Fat, ugly, and cheap." The Canadians say they spend as much money as anybody.

Rodin's famous statue, "The Thinker" has left France for the first time, as part of a touring exhibit in Asia. On the way back it will be dropped off at Hanford so workers can see what it looks like when you think.

Washington officials say the new jumbo ferry project could mean 500 to 600 more jobs for the state. That's good news for Puget Sound shipbuilders and the makers of cheap vodka.

When reporters asked Dan Quayle if he had any last words, he replied simply, "Goodbye: g-o-o-d-b-i."

Shawn Kemp has been invited to participate in the NBA All-Star Slam Dunk Contest, and Dana Barros will be in the Three-Point Shootout. Benoit Benjamin will be part of the Best Posture On The Bench Contest.

Joseph Albertson, the supermarket founder, died this week at age 86. The funeral featured one of Albertson's longtime employees singing, "It's Joe Albertson's funeral, but the meat department is mine."

A column in the Arizona Daily Star, said that Husky Coach Lynn Nance could "take the fun out of Disneyland." Although Nance disagreed, Disneyland officials said that after a Nance visit in 1990, Mickey Mouse left in tears and Goofy had a panic attack.

McChord Air Force Base has been mentioned as a possible passenger runway to relieve pressure from Sea-Tac Airport. The only drawback will be that you can only fly to Baghdad.

Boeing will donate $7 million to Washington State University. The donation was made for "continuing to send us quality graduates who know how to sleep on the job."

A Vashon Island photographer arrested in Peru, ate his videotape because he thought it would be used as evidence against him. He said he ate the tape in small pieces, and that it tasted sort of like chicken.

Seattle parking officers are getting new, better-equipped scooters called "Go-4's." With the new scooters, officers say they'll be able to ticket cars much faster and be much more efficient in pissing people off.

(Dr. Pepper Schwartz) I remember my most un-favorite sketch where they made fun of me. There was a big controversy of me having a male nanny, which came out when I wrote my book on pure marriage and they did a sketch about what a bad mother I was.

(Nancy Guppy) I think I did one sketch that I wrote, and it wasn't very funny, and it was about Pepper Schwartz. It was a stupid bit. I remember when we were doing it I was thinking, This is mean. Not mean funny, just mean, and not funny. And it's cheap. She didn't like it, and who would?

(Bill Stainton) Yea, she was not a fan. I mean, it was in the news! It was probably unfair, but you're on every week and what she was doing was in the news. We were in our twenties and thirties and were given the keys to the candy store and there's no oversight really. I seem to recall having an uncomfortable phone conversation with Pepper Schwartz.

(Dr. Pepper Schwartz) I wrote them a nasty letter and they wrote me an apology and that was the end of it.

(Pat Cashman) I did a bit called Sluggy. I did, like, five Sluggies. The idea basically is that it's a sort of a send up of Ralphy and all those kinds of kid-with-a-pet movies, except this kid couldn't afford a puppy or a cat, so he dumped a slug out in the yard and made that his pet.

 I remember the very first one we did, I hired a little kid actor because I was so impressed with the movie A Christmas Story, and the Ralphy character, and so I found this actor kid, that he had round glasses, he looked like him a little bit and I said, "Oh, this kid will be great." So, his mom brings him to the TV station and we are going to go out and shoot this Sluggy thing, and I realized, "Oh, she thinks she is coming with us. No, I don't want that, I don't want her to see what we are going to put him through," so we pretend like our van is so full that we don't have any room for anybody, and she said, "Well, can I just follow you?" "No, we've got to go and do a little bit of scouting first," and I made all these lame excuses up. So then when she finally saw the piece and sees her kid rolling down a hill and landing into a bunch of trees, and we put the slug's sort of slime all over his face. So I was a little duplicitous to pull that one off.

(John Keister) One of my favorite sketches was one that we called the College Terminator. Pat plays the Terminator like Arnold Schwarzenegger and he visits a business meeting. This really hard-charged businessman comes in; he's got a gun trained with lasers and everything. I'm one of the businessmen in the meeting and I am like, "What is this?" He asks, "Are you Richard Davis?" I am, like, "Yes." He says, "I am here to kill you now," and I go, "Why?" and he goes, "Because you asked for it," and I go, "What are you talking about?" I am obviously very agitated; I never asked anybody to kill me and he says that he comes from the future in a place where they monitor college parties in 1983. "You made a vow," and it goes back and it shows all of us in the cast, we are all in long hair and I say, "If I ever become just some money grubbing corporate guy just kill me," and around the table, everybody is, "Yeah, if I ever vote for republican just kill me, if I ever do..."— all these things and so he systematically goes and kills everybody, except for the one member who is down in the basement smoking dope and hasn't taken on any responsibility.

(Bill Nye) I loved being Speed Walker.

(Joe Guppy) Like many people, I had observed many times over the years how silly those speed walkers look. Somehow the idea of a superhero came into mind and there it was. I liked the conceit that he couldn't move any faster than speed walking, but got the job done anyway. Also, I had originally planned on playing the role myself— but then realized that it had to be Bill Nye!

(Ed Wyatt) I remember Keister giving Nye about a week to come up with a new Speed Walker episode. Bill came to the meeting and all he had was, "I think it would be cool for Speed Walker to run around the bases at the Kingdome." Keister just about exploded, then proceeded (in his own Keister-esque way) to sketch out an entire bit in about 20 minutes.

(Bill Nye) I was a natural as a Microsoft engineer. I admit to laughing at my own jokes in Flyin' Low and Refrigerator Magnet

Theatre. I was okay as a street walking lawyer of Aurora Avenue. In that bit you really see what Steve Wilson can do.

(Jim McKenna) We did a fake commercial about Chopper 5. Our version involved two Hell's Angels with the KING news logos on their backs, sitting on their "Choppers," pointing menacingly at the camera with a tag line, "We'll get the news, just stay out of our face." I paid them each a bottle of their favorite hooch.

(Ed Wyatt) Bob wrote a sketch called Yelling at Whores, which was just a bunch of losers yelling out a window at prostitutes walking by. You know, they think they're very funny but they're actually the losers because they're yelling at prostitutes.

(Bob Nelson) Unfortunately, I wrote this one. I was making fun of frat-like behavior in the office. What would be the craziest thing they could do? "Wanna go yell at whores?" "Okay." It was mainly a commentary on that type of behavior.

(Tracey Conway) It's these guys, just regular office guys working on something and Keister comes in and he says something like, "Hey, what you're up to?" "I'm just finishing up the report." "Well the meeting doesn't start for a couple minutes yet, you want to go yell at whores?"

(John Keister) KING didn't have windows that would open, but I used to work at the Rocket magazine and I knew that there were windows and it was a really nice looking building, so we had Tracy and Nancy dressed as street walkers and there were these guys in business suits yelling, "Hey, whores!"

(Bob Nelson) Unfortunately we were yelling out of an office window right by a business where a lot of people were working and had their windows open.

(John Keister) We were right next to this florist and this florist is like, "Who is yelling at whores? What is this?" and then they look up and see a KING van.

(Bob Nelson) Somebody found out that it was KING-TV and they called the station. So the Program Director comes up to Bill Stainton and says, "I don't believe this, I know this isn't true, but I just gotta come up here and check. Some people are saying there are KING employees yelling, "You're whores!" out a window." Then he looked over at the show board and there's our little card saying Yelling at Whores on it.

(Ed Wyatt) I loved The Crappy Old Car show, where we made fun of the car shows coming to the Kingdome. We just drove around [town] and shot the worst cars we could find. Very simple, very straightforward, that's the kind of stuff I loved. Frenetic Pace was one that I won an Emmy for which is ludicrous; it's a minute-twenty-five sketch about really fast moving news. It's like, "Here's the news." "How's the weather?" "Pretty good, let's go to sports." The fact that it won an Emmy to me is hilarious. For my acceptance speech I said this was so long in the making, I nurtured this thing from the beginning.

(Lauren Weedman) I'd never written jokes before and I can still remember, there are two jokes that are so a part of my life that I still quote them. One was—Bob Nelson, who was everybody's beloved, sweet Bob Nelson—he did this parody on that book The

Top Ten Habits of Highly Successful People and he wrote this sketch called The Top Ten Habits of Highly Mediocre People, and the first habit of highly mediocre people is to call out, "Good enough!" and walk away. And that has been like the motto of my life because even when I get tempted, it became like a life changing quote for me. It was so genius. The second joke was this, they would give us a set up for a joke and we had to come up with the punch line, which I loved, it was like mad-libs. And it's hard, harder than I would have imagined. The set up was, "Cinnabon has decided to change its colors and they're changing their colors to pink and green..." and I think the punch line they decided to go with was..."The favorite colors of fat people." Every time I think of that I laugh, in spite of myself.

(Ralph Bevins) I wrote this one bit, I think it was the last season or so, I came up with an idea based on the Guides for Dummies books, and this was for people more stupid than dummies and it was called the Guide for F-ing Morons. It was a commercial parody so there were voice-overs where they actually had to say the F-word, but Pat refused to say it in case it somehow made it out somewhere, so I had to get someone else to voice it. We bleeped out everything between the F and G but you could tell what they were saying. So I sit down with Jay Cascio (Program Director) and he's like, "Yea, we're not going to run that." So apparently you can't say F-ing Morons even if you don't say it, even if it's alluded to. The bit wouldn't have been funny unless you said the F-word. The repetition of it is what's funny.

(Bill Stainton) It was really, really funny! That was the kind of thing that I would love to put on. I really wish we could have aired that. That would have been one of those groundbreaking pieces.

(Nancy Guppy) I loved Nature walk with Chuck. I wrote the first one and then everyone wrote them after that. It's all about that great contrast: nature and a guy who throws garbage and smokes.

(Matt Smith) For some reason Pat Cashman either couldn't do it or didn't want to do it, so Nancy called me.

(Nancy Guppy) In the end we got Matt Smith. He's Chuck. He was a great improviser and actor. I knew we had to have someone who would go all the way with it. I think Pat's too nice, he would have made it goofy, and Chuck had to be a jerk, and Pat's not a jerk.

(Pat Cashman) I would say to you that my favorite times on the show were when I got the live bits. There was one bit where I wanted do this really, really fast sales pitch guy. He's raising his right hand, left hand, right hand, left hand, holding up different products and it would go faster and faster and faster. We had interns who were handling these things and putting them in my hand and I'd lift them up, and the fun of it to me was it had to go really fast, so you couldn't believe that this guy was on to so many products this quick. So we tried it and rehearsed it and it never worked, it never ever worked. There was always some mix up or I drop something. It only worked one time and that's when we did it on the air, and so that to me, that's a highlight for me.

(Ed Wyatt) Dave Grohl loved to come on the show; Kim Thayil from Soundgraden was on the Lame List.

(John Keister) Dave Grohl was great. When we did Rock Star Fantasy, that's another bit that's one of my favorites, Dave Grohl was on that, and it was like one of those baseball camps that guys go to and they play with the stars and ours was a rock 'n' roll fantasy camp.

(Kim Thayil) Dave Grohl was there, myself, I think Mike McCready did that as well and we would host yuppie-middle aged rock tourists trying to live out their rock fantasies. We'd show guys how to play guitar, how to pose with it, how to make certain rock star faces.

(John Keister) We'd do these different scenes like, how to break a guitar, how to do this or that – that's another bit that I would say is one of my favorites.

(Jeff Gilbert) When John pulled me into the office to explain what the Lame List was, I was the one who came up with the kicker line, What's Weak this Week, and we got each other  instantly, because I'd always been a fan of his. He's got a dangerously dark sense of humor. I was pals with all these rock musicians before they were stars so I got him a whole bunch of people—some Soundgarden guys, some Pearl Jam guys, some Mudhoney guys. We tried to get some Alice in Chains guys but that got tough because their careers were already starting to launch. We did this one sketch called the Grunge that Stole Christmas where we rounded up as many local rock guys as we could. TAD,

Grunt Truck, Forced Entry, Bitter End, Panic, Love Battery, those were some of the metal guys. And John would pretty much pay us in beer.

(Joleen Winther Hughes) Which would be the still preferred mode of payment to this day.

(Jeff Gilbert) You can get any of these rock guys to do anything if you offer them free beer and John wasn't prepared for how much beer we could actually drink.

(Kim Thayil) It pretty much revolved around yelling, "Lame", and doing it with different inflections, but none of us are actors so that was a little bit weird.

(Jeff Gilbert) Almost Live! got kind of a cult status when it was on and it was on quite a while before John came up with the idea of tagging these musicians to come in. And not one person said no. Everybody was so into it. This was back before everyone was selling platinum records and touring the world. They were just doing it to have fun. We'd roll down to RCKCNDY at about 10:30 to 11 o'clock in the morning and we had a blast. Everybody would pull up in rusted cars and band vans or took a bus.

(Joleen Winther Hughes) RCKCNDY was like a nice open free venue to shoot and we have a lot of graffiti and stuff as decoration. So, yeah, so we were always real open to that. It's such a small community that everybody really just kind of helped each other out.

(Chris Ballew) We did the Lame List one time, which was super fun. It was us in the basement of Mo, this club on Capitol Hill that's now Neumos. It was us instead of the normal heavy metal guys. We were just goofing off.

(Jeff Gilbert) We'd get together and John would have us be talking to each other and then he'd yell out some phrases and we'd all turn to the camera and yell, "Lame!" We'd just be standing there, out on the street, people would be driving by and honking. Audiences really liked it because it showed the music scene in Seattle really had a good sense of humor. And all the music people loved Almost Live! and John Keister.

(Chris Ballew) We love, love, loved our hometown. We loved Seattle. So anything to be connected to the community and help out various shows I'm game for. I'm a big believer in taking care of your back yard. It's kind of an extension of that Pete Seeger model of environmentalism where you clean up your own back yard and if everyone did that then the whole world would get cleaned up. I liked pouring my energies into my own back yard and make that a more entertaining and fun place.

(Bill Stainton) The Lame List was Keister's idea. Here's a little inside story. Anytime you saw the Lame List on the show it means something else didn't work out. Like a sketch we were gonna do just fell apart. The  Lame List was our emergency go-to. Because we didn't have to shoot anything, all we had to do was write five jokes, and nobody had to perform them. It was just words on a screen and then footage of our head bangers saying, "Lame! Lame! Lame!" I remember Kim Thayil from Soundgarden, one of the biggest bands in the world, and he'd told me they'd just done a tour and at that time we were syndicated on Comedy Central and we ran a lot of Lame Lists on Comedy Central and Thayil told me it would really piss him off because he was getting recognized more for the Lame List than being in Soundgarden. All across the country, "Oh, you're the Lame List guy!" "No, I'm the lead guitarist for Soundgarden!"

(Kim Thayil) They would take the footage and keep re-editing it with new text so it ran for years and years. So basically we did something we thought was a one-off...but it kept going. Then they'd start rerunning episodes of Almost Live! well after it was out of production...and it would just go on and on. So what seemed like a one-off thing that you suffer the embarrassment or humiliation as well as the attention of being on TV, that whole thing passed and then suddenly it came back and wouldn't go away. And so twenty years later, "Oh no, that thing's still there." You start getting recognized by a different generation of people, not for the music you did but for the fact you're on TV regularly. They would recognize my face, they made the correct assumption I was in a local rock band, and the local rock bands of note for causal music fans would have been Nirvana and Pearl Jam because they were so huge, they were household names, so people would ask me if I was in Pearl Jam and I would say, "No", and they would go, "Are you sure? Are you in Nirvana? Are you the bass player in Nirvana?" "No." "Are you the drummer for Pearl Jam?" "No, I'm really not." And they thought I was pulling their leg or giving them crap and I said, "Positive." Then they'd say, "Well, okay..." Then they'd stare at me, come back and say, "Are you sure? I see you all the time on Almost Live!." And I'd say, "Yes, I am on Almost Live!"

(Jeff Gilbert) I have to give credit to John Keister, he was a big fan of the hard rock scene and the punk scene. He got it. He got all of it. And he got it way before a lot of people.

Nick and Ben from Death Cab for Cutie, along with Harvey Danger surrounding Associate Producer Hans-Eric Gosch.

Oh, yea, I remember that sketch!

- **Chihuly and Jones**
Clips of the exciting adventures of the glass blowing/crime fighting team of Chihuly and Jones during a PBS beg-a-thon.

- **Steve Wilson vs Kenny G**
Kenny G's world record for longest note is challenged by Steve. The suspense is almost unbearable.

- **The Capitulator**
Need a super hero? Hope you don't get this one, whose super power is the incredible ability to give up. Oh, and don't forget his sidekick Back Down Boy. Pat Cashman and Joel McHale in tights.

- **Jus' Pimpin**
Brooks McBeth and Joel McHale as True Playaz on a public access program. Think Vanilla Ice turned up to 11.

- **Blizzard '96**
A retrospective on when a few flakes hit the ground and panic ensued.

- **Tough, hard, thorny issues**
Pat Cashman hosts this hot-button-topic talk show taking aim at the media's approach to racial reporting. Of course, the show is constantly interrupted with breaking news reports of such high urgency as a newspaper stolen from the porch of a home on Mercer Island and car antenna's being broken in Magnolia.

Cops in Leavenworth

Lame List Topics

- Parole Officers who aren't flexible
- Those guys in Nirvana pretend they don't know us anymore
- That Lynnwood woman who found $50,000 in a ditch and turned it in
- Bed frames that squeak
- Cops who can't take a joke
- Forty-year old guys with pony tails
- Bands moving to Seattle to get a record contract
- Jobs that start in the morning
- R movies with no nudity
- Zipper injuries
- Vanilla Ice
- Waking up in the yard
- Broken Slurpee machines
- Woodinville
- Foamy kegs
- Jeff Smulyan dating Monica Hart
- Guys in bands that sell a million records still bum beer money off of you
- Penile enlargements not covered by Blue Cross
- Your mom wants to borrow your girlfriend's thong bikini
- You just paid twenty bucks for a gram of parsley
- The great taste of beer without the alcohol

Quiz Programs

This was a short interstitial bit, simply text on screen. A question was posed and then there were several two-choice options. The correct answer was then marked.

Example:

- European Sports Term or Slang for getting sick?
  Korf (Team) Toss (Sick) Hurl (Team) Blow (Sick)

- Historical figure or Tennis pro?
- European coin or Non-sensical gibberish?
- Exotic dish or African City?
- Mass murderer or Sitcom neighbor?
- French wine or Hockey player?
- Biblical figure or County in Utah?
- Typographical error or Town in Wales?
- Famous spy or Sound you make when out of breath?
- Fancy hotel or Prep school cheerleader?
- Fashion model or Small Middle East nation?
- Baseball Hall of Famer or Expensive dinner?
- X-rated performer or Tasty cookie?
- Legal term or Roman leader?
- Olympic athlete or Meaningless phrase?
- Polaroid camera or Famous person's horse?
- Fresh water fish or Famous Chef?
- Baby talk or Food mart?
- College nickname or Thing in the ocean?
- Rap star or Type of gum?
- Pitcher nickname or Comment before sex?
- Fairy tale character or American fascist?

The Secret of their Success

A local comedy show airing for 15 years is beyond preposterous. That kind of thing simply doesn't happen. So that naturally begs the question, "How in heaven's name did Almost Live! last that long?" I asked the cast and a few other local celebrities. And journalists. And a professor. And an historian. And a sociologist.

(Steve Wilson) I look at when Ross was on as a completely separate show. Then there was the Lost Boys period and then when we got to the Saturday night slot that's when we really took off.

(Bob Nelson) It was nice when management just ignored us. I think it worked out in our favor that we were the crazy kids in the basement.

(Darrell Suto) KING kind of left it alone. The weird thing about the show was you would never, ever want to plan what we did. If you tried to have a local TV station sit down and figure out how to have a hit local TV show, they would come up wrong. Originally it was the standard TV model: a talking head, you sit behind a desk and interview people. That's how the show started. It's the easiest thing, you've got four cameras in a studio, you've got a whole crew you're already paying for anyway, you'd just put them out there and shoot. Whomever's in town you'd put them on there, get a funny bit and there you go.

(Feliks Banel) We were so spoiled with local TV in this area. We just had this good luck of having some really awesome, talented, smart, well-done local programming and not everyone in the country had that. Especially heading into the '90s. By that time a lot of places were already flipping over to syndicated programming. Why take the risk of running a local sketch comedy show? There's a lot of risk involved in that. They could have easily not done that. The fact that the show survived the sale of KING-TV from the Bullitt era to Provenance Journal era and then into the Belo era is pretty remarkable.

(Bill Stainton) We touched a nerve. I know when I took over the show I was thinking, I'll be in Seattle for the next three years, if we don't completely F it up maybe we'll get five years out of this. I mean, a local comedy show, come on. But I think a few things happened. First of all, I think once we switched to a half an hour and were able to get that time slot all of a sudden we had this one-two punch of us and Saturday Night Live. That was a shot of adrenaline. It was the perfect timing. If we'd stayed on Sundays at six we would have been off the air after another year or two.

(Nancy Guppy) I think the percentage of the material being funny was high enough. The local angle was huge. People who liked the show loved knowing what we were making fun of. They loved knowing Kent and Ballard and Lynnwood, Tacoma and Mercer Island. It's like those places were so unique and distinct at that time, they really did have a personality. The stereotypes were true. It's comedy so we just turned up the heat on it. Also, it was the right group of people at the right time.

(Darrell Suto) It was this perfect storm of people.

(John Keister) We had a unique combination of people that it just worked; we didn't really look like a traditional comedy show, we had a lot of everyman, everywoman. We looked like regular people but we really knew how to write comedy and we really knew how to produce comedy.

(Tracey Conway) I would say that, if we were lucky, ten percent of the stuff we put on the air was really funny. But for the people who were putting that show together, a small group of people, and getting it on the air, twenty-three, twenty-four times a year, I think we did a great job.

(Feliks Banel) What distinguished the JP Patches show and Almost Live! was the creativity and the talent required—to write, in the case of Almost Live!, and to perform, in the case of Chris Wedes (JP). Almost Live! was able to take that sketch comedy convention that goes back to vaudeville, they took what they had and made the most of it. The same way Wedes and Newman (Bob Newman—i.e. Gertrude) would get up every day with no budget, have a cup of coffee and talk about what the show was going to do that day, Almost Live! was able to take this shoe string budget and do brilliant stuff with it because they had their great ideas, funny writing and for the most part really good performing.

(Steve Wilson) It was also a late night show so it catered to a younger crowd, particularly males 18-30 years old. That's a key market. The beer drinking market, the pizza buying market. That's a huge coup.

(Erik Lacitis) You could sit around in your living room [watching] with your college buddies and not feel bad that you didn't have a date that night.

(Dave Kreig) I used to watch it and wish I could be on it. I thought it was so innovative and so funny. I just thought it was the coolest thing.

(Dave Wyman) I used to watch it every night before we played home games. My ritual was to watch Almost Live! and then SLN.

I would wake up at 8:30 and that seemed to be a winning combination (7 ½ hours of sleep was just right). I would talk about it in the locker room the next day and pretty soon other guys started watching it too and lines from Almost Live! were often used in Seahawk locker room humor.

(Dan Lewis) I was on several times. They mentioned me a lot. I wasn't mentioned as much as Ballard or Kent but my hair did get quite a bit of attention. There would be a lot of times where I would come in to work and my co-workers would say, "They got you again."

(Steve Raible) Anytime you're in local television, it's a much more difficult business now, certainly, than it was in those days, but there are so few stations, not only in this market, but stations around the country that were doing local programming that was not news-based. And so to do a show that was so thoroughly off the track of newscasts or typical programming that are based on the news department; that was unusual. And, quite frankly, it was remarkable that it was on that long, although it should be no surprise because the Bullitt family and KING realized that this was one of those [shows] that differentiated from everybody else, not only in this market but in the entire county. It was always fun to look up and see that show and think, "Hey, I know some of those guys." And look at some of them now, they've gone on and done great things.

(Steve Wilson) Because of the way Seattle was growing in the public eye and because when we were kids there would be local columnists like Jean Godden or Emmett Watson, you'd read those guys every day because they talked about stuff that was the flavor of the town. They really captured the essence of what the city was about, and that's what we did. We made it funny.

(Marty Riemer) Seattle has always had this west coast, we're-not-worthy attitude and prior to Almost Live! they would have said we're not big enough to have idiosyncrasies that we can make fun of that everyone gets. And Almost Live! gave us that. It gave us unique things about Kent and Ballard that we could laugh at. It made the city feel like a bigger metropolis as a result. I don't think Seattle at that time felt like there were things here that could really be made fun of; we were too podunk, we were an outpost. And Almost Live! said, "Dammit, no, we're a big city."

(Erik Lacitis) The show bridged both worlds of Seattle. Seattle was getting bigger; it was getting more...new arrivals to the Northwest. I think Seattle still thinks of itself as a town where we have Seafair and hydro races, so when I say that it bridged, the humor—sharp, biting humor—it was never mean—it took what Seattle used to be to what Seattle was becoming.

(Bob Nelson) People would ask me, "How can you do a show on Comedy Central? How are they going to get the Ballard and Kent jokes?" Almost half of our material wasn't locally oriented, but that's what people remember. I always thought the key to that was John Keister and before that with Ross, the two of them were from the Northwest and when I joined the show, we really depended on John's sensibility. I think John's knowledge of local history was one of the key ingredients.

(Steve Wilson) What the show did best was we defined the neighborhoods. Now they've been redefined since, but we defined Ballard as where all the old people live, Kent where all the hicks live, Lynnwood where all the women with the blue eye-shadow live, Bellevue, the rich people. Keister had his finger on that really well.

(Feliks Banel) He understands a lot about Seattle culture that goes far beyond just a sketch comedy show. He's also sort of a sweet, sentimental guy, which I don't think comes across unless you realize that his humor was his way of professing his love for the region and of the quirkiness that we used to have.

(John Keister) Yeah, I certainly did and one of the reasons for that was that I was shown an awful lot of love and support early on the show when people would come up to me on the street, "We really like you!" But then when I took over and I wasn't doing very well as a host, I was like, well, when is the big backlash going to come? But that didn't happen. It was strange that it didn't happen and then when things finally turned around and the show started doing well I thought, I don't know that there is any place like this in show business. I felt like there was just a lot of support for me. When things started going well I really felt like I had a debt to the people here.

(Tracey Conway) I think it was a Valentine to the Northwest. We loved where we lived. We loved to poke fun at it and basically we just loved it.

(Joe Guppy) The one thing that people loved about Almost Live! is that it preserved that local humor and that old Seattle feel.

(Steve Raible) It did such a great job of skewering those of us here in the Northwest. I thought it was terrific.

(Dori Monson) They created characters and recurring bits that everybody talked about. I miss the fact that we don't have local TV that creates buzz like Almost Live! did, that gave us the cultural touchstones that you don't find in local TV anymore.

(Bill Nye) We had all fallen into roles, so we had bits we could count on: Mind Your Manners with Billy Quan, The Lame List, The Worst Girlfriend in the World, Urban Wildlife, and Speed Walker. It's easier to write just the comedic scenarios with such solid characters and formats already in place than to create new characters from whole cloth. It freed up guys like Pat Cashman, Ed Wyatt, and especially Bob Nelson to create new amazing things that would just kill.

(Bill Stainton) We got better and better at what we were doing. We also offered a perspective on things that nobody else could offer. I used to hear this a lot of times from people who moved to Seattle, they said they learned about Seattle through us, which is true because we were the shorthand. We dealt in stereotypes.

(Dr. Pepper Schwartz) There were enough stereotypes to be true. It's like the Pemco insurance ads: The guy who wears sandals and socks. The guy who won't cross the street at three in the morning unless it says Walk. It's all the things that are not true of everybody but are just true enough. They used to do a lot of sketches about neighborhoods and it made those neighborhood people feel observed and important enough to be made fun of.

(Dori Monson) They created a community around here. It was unique; it was fun. The characters were memorable. It was like JP Patches, the same sort of vibe.

(Tony Ventrella) People don't mind being made fun of a little. And quite frankly, they were right about Kent and Ballard.

(Dr. Pepper Schwartz) We were cool enough to be made fun of!

The VHS videotape sleeve. Back when there was VHS.

(Feliks Banel) Keister and those guys were so brilliant in their observational comedy—Ballard Vice is brilliant—the way they made fun of the distinct neighborhoods, and they were much more distinct back then, it's a great mirror to hold up, you can look back and look at the jokes about Boeing engineers and Microsoft jokes, it's probably a better way to understand that period than going back and reading the newspaper.

Almost Live

(Dr. Pepper Schwartz) They had some quirky characters and Seattleites like quirk. I think we had the conceit that we had our own Saturday Night Live and that we could chuckle about ourselves, that we were the insiders on a joke. It made us a community in a way because of the city and because of these characters. They weren't always funny but they were always interesting.

(Dave Kreig) It made me so much more aware of the city and the little communities around it. They talk about stuff like the ferries and I'm from a little town in Wisconsin and I'm like, "Ferries?"

(Erik Lacitis) If I had been a newcomer to the area I would have watched because it told you what this town's history was about.

(Feliks Banel) The local stuff they did, it was a great window to look into that era that you could not get from looking at Seattle Times articles. That kind of thoughtful creativity and satire, that's such a great way to very quickly understand what was important in a certain era or what people liked or didn't like.

(Dave Wyman) It was a great way to get to know the city. I felt like the local humor was so great. I started mentioning it around the locker room and before long other players started watching it. I remember before a game, me, Dave Kreig, Mike Tice and one other white guy were standing around and Jacob Green came up said, "Hey, can I be a high-five'n white guy?" And of course we'd all look at him and say, "Noooooooooo."

(Tony Ventrella) Quality comedy survives. But I don't know if we have the forward thinking executives who would give it a shot because it's not like the old days. Back in the day when the Bullitt's owned the station the Program Director might say,

"Here's an idea, let's give that a shot." Today you wouldn't even talk about that until you first talk about sponsorship. I mean, if Howard Schultz suddenly stepped up and said, "Here's ten million, let's put Almost Live! back on the air for a few years," you would suddenly have a Program Director who would go, "You know what? Almost Live! would be a good idea." It's all about the dollars now.

(Dan Lewis) It was so creative and unique. I'm a huge believer in local programming and as the years go on we see less and less of it and they took a huge chance to do local comedy and they had talented people. I was always impressed with the effort they put into it.

(Dr. Pepper Schwartz) A sense of humor *is* sociology. You have to understand whom you're talking about at a fairly refined level so that there's a group recognition and a group self-satire. And that means you have to be very aware of all of the things that we all share, how do we feel about them, what do we all find amusing and what do we all want to stick a pin in, what the boundaries are—what's funny bad taste versus hitting a nerve and nobody's laughing. You have to know how much you can push and get people uncomfortable to get people amused and how much push before they want to get rid of you. You have to understand people and what are those everyday life things that we enjoy. To be a good comedian you have to be smart and have to be a sociologist, even if you weren't trained to be one.

(Dr. John Findlay) Seattle was growing like crazy and becoming more sophisticated and getting a lot of national attention and here's this show that's taking this city that's very cosmopolitan and taking the areas that are more provincial and laughing at itself.

The show was awfully white. I mean they even make fun of that with the High-Five'n White Guys who aren't cool.

(Steve Wilson) Well, we certainly couldn't do any race humor because we didn't have any people of color on the staff.

(Pat Cashman) I think we could have done a better job of that.

(John Keister) The audience complained about it, and yes, I would be shopping and I would frequently have black people say, "You know, I don't understand why, explain to me why this show isn't this way." The answer, I said, is because there wasn't anybody in the office at the time when the show was made. If there had been somebody [of color] we would have put that person on the air. People a lot of times erroneously think that KING decided to have some auditions to bring people on, but that isn't the way it worked. We never – no one ever said, "Hey, let's do a comedy show and we want like, let's see, we will have a white guy, a woman, a black guy..." that typical ensemble cast.

(Pat Cashman) I think the effort to bring more color onto the show was earnest. But a full-time cast member would have meant the dismissal of someone already in the cast, I suppose.

(Steve Wilson) We had a set number of people that we could have on the staff. If one person left then we had a hole to fill.

(Pat Cashman) I really do think that the effort was always to acquire the best writers and comedic actors that could be found— and ethnicity wasn't a major criterion at the time. When the show began, it was much more contemporary with Kids in the Hall, Monty Python and the like—where all-white casts were fortunately or unfortunately so much the norm. When the show ended in 1999, it was already becoming more inclusive of other races and cultures—with at least two semi-regular black cast members and a pair of additional female cast members added to the troupe.

(Ed Wyatt) Seattle's demographic was pretty white. In the city and on the airwaves. In fairness, if you look back at our sketches, we did have some minority performers at times - Dave Huddleston, Enrique Cerna, those guys helped us out a bit. Kim Evey, who is Asian American, came along after I was gone. Trust me, if we had the budget for an African American actor we would have hired someone in a heartbeat. We watched Saturday Night Live and other shows—we knew we were heavily white.

(Nancy Guppy) It was a very white city and a white show. It was definitely on people's minds. What it came down to was can [this person] write? That was always the main thing.

(Bill Stainton) My policy was to always hire writers who could perform—in that order. To me, the writing was the paramount skill. And, unfortunately, I didn't have the budget to have a writing staff and an acting staff. They had to be the same people. I used to get writing submissions all the time. And I can tell you that 99% of those submissions came from white guys in their '20s. Not women. Not ethnic minorities. (And, of course, of all the submissions I got over the years, most were crap, which diminished the odds even further.) My dream was always to find a brilliant black female writer who could perform. It would have really expanded our range on the show! Maybe I didn't look hard enough, or in the right places, but I never found the right person. Kim Evey (Asian) was an extremely talented actress—I'm not sure why I didn't hire her.

(Nancy Guppy) There was a guy named David Scully and he was on the show a lot and he could write and he was an outstanding performer so he was with the show for a while, but there probably wasn't a slot for a permanent person, and really, if anyone was to be the person to take someone else's place it probably would have been David.

(John Keister) We brought some people on who were really, really good but the uncomfortable thing is that when a position opened up that we could hire another member on the show, there was this discussion that obviously it had to be someone of color, and then we auditioned a bunch of people, and then it was like, "So we are *not* going to hire Joel (McHale)? It's not going to be Joel?" And it was like, "No, it's going to be Joel." That probably wouldn't have been tolerated today.

(Dr. John Findlay) The show reflects a Seattle that's maybe not as multi-cultural or as sensitive to multi-cultural dimensions of the city as would be the case today, so in some ways it's a relic. Doesn't mean it wasn't influential. What's ironic is that they did bits where they made fun of Seattle's political correctness.

Oh yea, I remember that sketch!

- **Boeing Contract Negotiations**
What it takes to get the machinists union back at it. A tractor pull, monster trucks, and a dollar off all King beers at the Kingdome? Deal. Okay, not quite.

- **Spring Break at Alki**
Wearing parkas and scarves just doesn't seem to have the same appeal as what you might see in Fort Lauderdale.

- **Carnival Ride Operator Institute**
You can be working the lucrative carnival circuit in less than two months. Every week you'll travel to a thrilling new destination, like Aberdeen.

- **Flyin' Low**
A favorite of Boeing pilots. Starring Bill Nye and Ed Wyatt as Captain Flanker and Jeff Dawson—A couple of guys whom like to take chances and see the world up close. They inevitably crash. Every time.

- **Urban Sportsman**
Hunting yuppies and mimes on the streets of Seattle. Somebody's gotta do it.

- **WSU Orientation**
Students have a hard time understanding the concept of a dry campus. They presume that Bud Dry is okay. They wonder if there's any reason to be in a fraternity anymore.

Recognition has its Perks

If you're in show biz you like fame. Hmm, perhaps that's too broad a generalization. Maybe it's safer to say if you're in show biz you like recognition. That's the nature of performers—to be recognized and appreciated for their craft. Applause is catnip to any entertainer worth his or her salt. What most celebrities don't like is the negative consequences of fame—being stalked by paparazzi, people after your money, jealousy, etc. That was one of the beauties of being on Almost Live!. The cast became locally famous—household names for many of them—but their fame, at least for most of them, didn't extend beyond a 300-mile radius, and therefore they weren't movie star/rock star famous. Just kind of, "Hey, that's John Keister! Cool. Hey John, how you doing?" famous. That level of fame was flattering and comfortable. Did they occasionally get pestered to the point of annoyance? Yea, but usually not. It's Seattle after all. You know the show's popular when not just the cast but the crew got a little love.

(Bob Nelson) We didn't really know [our popularity] for the first two or three years. It took a while for it to reach that status. I think the first time I realized something was up was when, I think it was in the spring of '93, we were asked to play a charity basketball game at a high school against the teachers. The gym was packed and it did feel like a rock concert. People were just screaming. I think I suddenly realized we do have a pretty rabid following.

(Ross Shafer) I remember my kids were young and I would get stopped a lot to take pictures, people would want me to sign autographs, I started wearing a fake mustache and a wig when I was with my kids so that I try not to get bothered.

(Bill Nye) I was recognized often enough, nothing like the way John was. After the Science Guy show started airing, things got busy for me in public. I left Seattle in part to get away from being so recognizable and accessible. I was dining at a small restaurant one evening with Darrell Suto, and a stranger just pulled a chair up to our table, started talking— and wouldn't leave. It was before selfie photos. People's fascination with those of us on television was captured well by [a sketch that John did] of John driving around and getting stuff for free— because he was on TV.

(John Keister) Basically whatever we asked for people gave us because they liked to be associated with the show, they would like to have their name on the credits. But the other thing was that they knew who we were and so there was no anxiety about, we know where to find you. I mean it's like, if we needed, like, a Mercedes to drive around because we needed to play a rich character, the Mercedes people would go, "Oh yeah!" They would just let us drive a car around and bring it back. See, the thing is, people train you to do that, it's not like you are walking in like you are some big shot and say, "Hey, I want this," you go in and you're like, at a restaurant, and you go, "I am…" and they stop you and they say, "I know who you are," like they are upset that you would think they wouldn't know who you are. And so then they go, "Yeah, we have got a table for you right over here," and after a while you stop saying what your name is because you have been trained, you don't even really notice that you are doing it, you just walk into the Met and say, "I need a table," and they are like, "Right over here," and you just start living life that way and you don't notice it, you don't really notice it.

(Ross Shafer) When John and his wife were having their babies I had already gone to Hollywood and there had been lot of press about it. John and [his wife] were having an emergency where she has got to get to the hospital and it's a breach and it's very difficult and they can't get hold of their doctor. When they get to the admitting room in the hospital the woman says, "We need some more paperwork." John said, "I don't have any more paperwork, my wife is going to die in your room with these two babies, we can't get hold of the doctor." He is freaking out, and finally this woman said, "Fill out this form." And he had to fill out a form at this crisis moment, and he fills out and he turns it around and the nurse looks at him and he goes, "John Keister, oh my god! Hey, what's Ross doing these days?"

(Steve Wilson) At first when we were getting really popular we decided to go to a bar and watch the show. So we'd finish the show at 10 o'clock and then meet down at the Brooklyn. Pretty soon word got out that, hey, this is where they have their after-party. So we'd get down there and the place was packed. So soon they pitched us and said, "Hey, if you keep coming down here we'll comp all your drinks and food."

(John Keister) The other thing is you feel really safe. This actually happened to me where I was in Columbia City and there are gang members and they are like, "Hey, you are the guy from TV," and I go, "Who you are guys?" and they are like, "We are the Crips," and I am like, "Oh! I have always wanted to meet the Crips," and they are all in blue and stuff, I go, "I really like your guys' color better than the Bloods," and they are like, "Yeah, that red is too loud." They actually said that to me. So stuff like that would happen but I would say the epitome of that was when I had a tape deck stolen out of my car and so I am driving away from home and my wife says, "How are you going to get to work?" And I go, "Well, there will be somebody there – someone will take me to work." and I drove my car up to Magnolia Hi-Fi, dropped it off and I run across the street and I just stood at the corner and a car pulled over and said, "What are you doing here?" And I said, "Would you take me to work?" And they are like, "Yeah, get in," and I knew that that would happen. [People] just wanted to be part of the show, part of the experience and you get trained into that and then if you go to some other city where people don't know you, you're suddenly like, at night, you get, "Oh man, I am not safe here." I never felt unsafe in Seattle during that time.

(Ed Wyatt) I remember when we went to Vancouver to shoot the High-Five'n White Guys. We were really, really well known in Vancouver because the show was on the air there. The highlight was when John took us to a strip club and we're all sitting around watching and a girl does some acrobatic thing and ended up right in front of John and looked up and realized who it was and said, "I know you!" It was fantastic!

(John Keister) Yeah, I love the strip clubs in Vancouver, and yes that did happen.

(Mike Boydstun) Keister seemed to know all the names of the strip clubs. Razzmatazz was just a few blocks away from KING, right by the Elephant car wash, and they had this marquee reader board out front that they would change, kind of like the funny little sayings they would have at the old Lusty Lady by the art museum. Well John and I were driving by and we see the sign and it says, "Raz girls love Keister's keister," and John is like, what?

(Matt Smith) I did the sketch Nature Walk with Chuck, which only aired four times. I'm an auctioneer for a living and I'll have someone staring at me, they can't figure out how they know me, and finally they'll go, "It's Chuck!"

(Tracey Conway) I will definitely say I met some really interesting gents because they knew me from the show and I dated a few of them, one of them for a while. Man, if Internet dating had been available then.

(Darrell Suto) One time I was flying to another city and I'd slept in and was late for my flight and I'm running into Alaska Airlines, absolutely sweating because I was going to a meeting that was really important, and there's, like, ten minutes before the plane leaves and I run up and say, "Can I still get on that plane?" And they're like, "Billy!" And then everyone has to come over and I'm thinking, Okay, I really need to go now.

(Bill Stainton) [The recognition] was a double-edged sword, it got to the point where I couldn't go into a local comedy club because all the comics would come up and say, "Hey, why don't you have me on the show?" Here's one time that really pissed me off. I went into some bar and somebody came up to me and said, "Are you guys shooting a bit? Because John Keister was just here and everyone was buying him drinks." And I'm like, "Oh, okay." And I wait, and nobody buys me a drink. Everybody's buying John Keister a drink, hey, I'm on the same show, I'm the one who made him the goddamn host! But no, not a single drink offer and it really pissed me off.

(Joe Guppy) I loved being Mr. Nancy Guppy. I loved her being popular. I've often said, by the time I left Seattle I was kind of a minor celebrity, everywhere I went I was recognized and people would talk to me. And then when I return from LA I'm a nobody, so it was cool that I got to experience both. And I discovered that I prefer the not being recognized. But when I hang around with Nancy I get to get the best of both worlds.

(Tracey Conway) I still will meet people who say, "I've loved you for years," but it's like, I always feel like I'm going to disappoint people with who I really am with the image of who they think I might be.

(Ralph Bevins) It was exciting to be associated with the show. I didn't want to go around broadcasting that I worked for the show but I was always hoping that someone would ask me who I worked for. Just last week I went out to see one of John (Keister's) shows and John said hi to me, and somebody in line said, "Oh, you know John Keister?" And I'd say, "Oh, I shot for the show," and this woman says, "I just want to thank you so much." That was a really unique experience because you don't get people thanking the camera guy.

(Matt Smith) It was funny walking around with Keister; he said half the people liked him. If they honked there was a fifty-fifty chance they'd say, "Hey man, I love you," or, "You (bleep), you dumb (bleep), you're not funny." He would have to sometimes introduce a big act and he'd have to have two things ready, one if they cheered him and one if they booed him. And he took it all in stride.

(John Keister) Right, yeah, in particular with Jerry Seinfeld when I was going to introduce him, he was on this big tour at the height of his popularity and I was really worried to go out there and introduce Jerry Seinfeld because it was like, all these people out there going, "We don't want to see this local guy, we want to see Jerry Seinfeld." It was just the opposite, I got this huge roar of approval from the crowd and then when I went backstage before he went on, he looked at me, "They sure know you in this town."

(Steve Wilson) Christmas Eve, my then girlfriend, Kim, and I were looking to do something different so we go down to the Metropolitan Grill to have a drink. It's, I dunno, maybe ten o'clock at night and there's one other couple in the bar. So the bartender delivers our martinis and says, "Compliments of the gentleman and his girlfriend right there." And I look down and nod thank you, and I look and it's Chris Kattan from Saturday Night Live. I go, "Oh my god, are you Chris Kattan?" He goes, "Yea." I said, "I'm a big fan of yours," and he says, "I'm a big fan of *yours*!" He grew up on Bainbridge Island, he still goes back there; his mom still lives there, and we just sat there and had this mutual admiration society and he talked about bits that he loved from Almost Live!. That was one of the coolest nights of my life. I mean, he sent me a drink, for god sakes.

(John Keister) When Almost Live! was on Comedy Central all the young comics watched, I mean everybody watched everybody else's show and so I visited Saturday Night Live because I had some friends who worked there, and people like Mike Myers, he said that he really liked it. I get messages from them and from other comics and other people in show business that they really enjoyed the show and later when Bob (Nelson) was working on Nebraska and Bob Odenkirk was one of the characters in Nebraska, he at one point said, "You know, for a script that's kind of this dark there is a lot of humor in this," and they said, "Well, Bob used to work on a comedy show," and he was like, "What's that? Almost Live!?" He was like, "Oh! I know that, yeah, I watched that show," and Bob was just filming another movie that Patton Oswalt was in, and Patton Oswalt was like, "Yeah, I remember I used to watch you playing – doing Uncle Fran and stuff like that."

(Bill Stainton) Michael Jordan knew about the show. A lot of celebrities were like this. They'd come into Seattle for a game or something like that, Saturday night they go back to their hotel, they'd tune in to watch SNL and they'd be, "What the hell's this thing?" And they liked it, so apparently word got around the NBA, "Hey, if you're in Seattle you should check this show out." So it was a nice surprise when Michael Jordan knew about the show when we asked him to do a short bit. It was always tough approaching celebrities who didn't know the show, like one time I asked Cindy Crawford and she turned me down, which didn't do anything to help my self-esteem.

(Ross Shafer) My job now is that I write business books and I lecture on them. I'm kind of a funny motivational speaker based on the research I do for my books. Just recently I was in the Dominican Republic speaking to a very large business. There were probably about 500 people there and after I finish a guy comes up and says, "Can I get my picture with you?" I say, "Sure," and he's got his arm around me and he says, "Man I loved you on Almost Live!." So even to this day, some 30 years later there's still something that struck a chord with people and that TV show. You just never know when you're talking into that little lens where it's going.

1997

- Princess Diana killed in car crash.
- Microsoft becomes world's most valuable company.
- Mike Tyson bites Evander Holyfield's ear.
- Harry Potter and the Sorcerer's Stone published.
- Voters approve funding for Seahawks' new stadium.

1998

- Benaroya Hall opens.
- Metro bus plunges 50 feet off Aurora Bridge when passenger shoots driver.
- President Bill Clinton denies he had sexual relations with Monika Lewinsky. Cue punch lines.
- Google is founded.
- Apple unveils the iMac.

The Newbies

Almost Live! was the proverbial odd duck; an anomaly in sketch comedy. Cast members would come on and stay on. It wasn't a revolving door of talent. Very little turnover. But in the last couple of years they broke form and purposefully rotated in new cast members to keep it fresh and to see who might stick.

It was a risk. Bring in the wrong person and chemistry can go south fast and audiences will abandon ship in short order.

As it turns out their eye for talent hadn't diminished.

(Matt Smith) Towards the end they wanted to add more diversity to [the show]. They wanted younger people and people of color to make the show more representative of Seattle.

(Lauren Weedman) They had sort of like guest spots, which were basically auditions. Joel [McHale] did it; I did it, Matt Smith. And then they chose from there.

(Matt Smith) So they invited I think eight different people, two at a time for seven weeks for the whole season. I did it with Laura Weedman.

(Lauren Weedman) I didn't know the show at all since I didn't grow up in Seattle but I'd done a film with John Keister the year earlier, it was called That Night, and everywhere we'd go shooting  people were losing their taters over John, and I'm, like, "So he's the hot guy in town, how lucky am I that I landed in Seattle and the first person I work with in theater is the only celebrity in town basically, other than JP Patches." He was such a big deal and so respected.

(John Keister) I really liked [Lauren], she wasn't exactly right for the lead in the film that I was doing but I thought her audition was so strong that I wrote an extra part because I wanted her in the film. I thought she would be a really good part of, like the best friend of the lead in the film and she really brought a lot to it.

(Lauren Weedman) I was not a sketch comedy person and I didn't consider myself a comedian but I really liked John and liked his whole background with his music interest and knowledge of Seattle, he knew so much  about it. He was this subversive, cool dude and I just liked hanging out with him. So when I was on the show I had a lot of really alternative friends and they all thought they were so hipster and all my theater folks that they're friends with are, like, "Oh my god, Almost Funny, you're gonna be on Almost Funny? That show is past its prime." They were all really young, early twenties, way too cool, but when I got the opportunity to be on the show, as soon as I got that job they're all, "Um, if they ever need an extra…" And a couple of my friends who were used on the show, I know it was a big deal to them because it was the only game in town. So I was caught in two worlds because I loved being on the show and for me it was an amazing opportunity being on camera because I had never done that and to be in such a straight up professional environment, well professional may be a little strong, but I was paid and I was on salary.

(Bill Stainton) Lauren Weedman never really fit in with the group because she was really a solo performer and so when she would write something it would be basically a Lauren Weedman monologue with the rest of us as an audience. She had a quirkiness that made me a little uncomfortable, but John loved it.

(Lauren Weedman) For me it was a hard year because I wanted to be succeeding and it was stressful, and I felt lucky to be part of that. And I also new I wasn't what people wanted. I was really aware that the fans of Almost Live! did not want to see a new girl. I stuck out for sure I think. I like to think I didn't kill Almost Live! but…

(Joel McHale) I was doing tons of theater; I was doing football and tons of theater downtown at Unexpected Productions and doing theater at the University of Washington. And then I did an internship at Almost Live! and I did an internship with Pat Cashman. I was a terrible student but I loved sports and I loved acting so I was doing pretty much everything except for school.

(Pat Cashman) There are interns that just jump out, and Joel McHale was one of them. These guys, from the moment they arrive are like, "Can you show me how to edit stuff?" and, "How do you, like, do these things?" and then they want to know everything.

(Nancy Guppy) Joel and I really bonded really early on and I knew that he had something. Joel was an intern and If interns came on and pushed for anything beyond being an intern you didn't like it. It was like, "Just be an intern, all right? We'll find out if you're  good or not." Joel never did. He was goofy, funny, had great stories, really fit in really well, and he just kind of meshed. He was the right person at the right time.

(John Keister) I mean he had all the tools. He was great comedically and people just—there were certain people who were able to punch through the screen that people really like and he was one of those people.

(Hans-Eric Gosch) When I joined Almost Live! following my time as an NBC Page at 30 Rock I was ten years younger than anyone else on the show. In turn I found myself in front of the camera on most weeks whenever they needed to cast anyone who could almost pull off a college-age person. When Joel McHale joined the show a few seasons later as an intern he began playing those parts and completely killed it. Joel was great right away and was asked by Bill Stainton in short order to join the cast. Bill Stainton is the secret sauce of Almost Live! and great at recognizing talent, but everyone noticed Joel's talent right away.

(Pat Cashman) He is not just a good actor, a funny guy and all of that stuff, but he is a really great human being. I started getting these letters at the radio station, and at first they were kind of charming, they were handwritten and they  say, "Hi Pat, my name is so-and-so and I would like, you know, I think it would be cool if it was just you and me and John Keister, that we have an apartment together, then we could watch movies and stuff and it would be real cool." I'm thinking, You know, that's cute, the little guy must be 11 or 12. Slowly over time, his letters started getting really dark, and creepier, and then I find, I think this guy is not a little kid, he is like a 25, 26 year old guy, and so I'm reading about all this stuff because he is actually threatening to kill me. Joel said, "You've got to take this to the police." I said, "No, I am not that worried about it." He said, "You should be."

(Joel McHale) They were truly bizarre. The only reason it's funny is because the guy didn't try something. He was obsessed with Pat.

(Pat Cashman) And so Joel decided he is going to just drive down to the guy, he was in Auburn or someplace, he was that dumb, he put his address on the envelope. Joel drives down there, he pulled up at the house and he sits and does surveillance of this guy who is living with his parents as it turns out. And he is a little, more than a little addle-brained, and Joel really watches him, and ultimately decided he is no big threat. But I mean he just did that independently.

(Joel McHale) I drove down there, because, what the hell? I was, like, 19, it was something to do.

(Matt Smith) Joel was a student of mine; I was one of his first teachers. I worked with him and this unbelievably great group of kids at Youth Theater Northwest on Mercer Island. And Joel had decided that he was going to go back to school and get his masters in acting. So basically he quit doing the show because he had bigger plans for himself. One thing about Joel was that he was a really amazing learner.

(Joel McHale) Matt Smith was one of my teachers in high school. He was great. I was very, very lucky in that there was a youth theater program on Mercer Island where I grew up that was really terrific. And there was a group of actors there that were remarkable. I learned so much from them, and then you had a teacher like Matt who was world-class. A lot of those people went on to have real big careers. There's a girl named Annie Parisse who was in that group, she was on Law and Order for years, Reiko Aylesworth was in that group, she was on 24, Dominic Deleo, who I still work with on The Soup, he's one of the writers, Ethan Sandler, he just wrote and starred in a pilot on AMC last year. The Youth Theater Northwest, where we all attended, is still very active on Mercer Island.

(Ed Wyatt) When I took the job as host of Good Evening in Portland we lost a guy and needed to fill a reporter position. Joel at the time was doing some stuff on Almost Live! but I don't know if they were paying him or not. I called Joel and said you should consider this. He flew down for the interview and they were blown away. When Keister got wind of that I think that's when they started paying Joel.

(Joel McHale) I was so young and the entire cast just took care of me. I'm totally dyslexic, and they will attest to how nervous I was for the live sketches and how I can't read. They will tell you how lousy I was. It was a great place, it was on local television and in a weird way it was a great place to break me in, to go, "Oh, he can't really do it yet, but we can let him F it up for a couple of years and let him work out some bad habits." It was the time of my life. I loved being on the show, I loved that time; it was great to be in Seattle. All those things I got to be a part of. I just felt so blessed.

The first time I saw Dana Carvey was on that show. I saw Joe Walsh on that show. Just to know Pat Cashman, he was one of my idols. Pat was like my television dad. The fact that I was interning for him and acting beside him was so thrilling. I was so in awe of him. And John Keister. I remember going to lunch with John Keister and, "I'm eating with John Keister, I can't believe this."

(Lauren Weedman) When we were on Almost Live! he was absolutely clear that he was going to move to LA and be on some

TV shows and be famous. "I'm going to go to town and work it and make it happen." I told him, "That's just not how it happens Joel, you have to suffer," but he was so exactly right.

(Bob Nelson) I think the thing you always wonder about anybody is, I see the talent, are they going to jump in and go for it, because it's one thing to be able to do it, it's another thing to make the decision that you're going to uproot yourself and go to LA and go through all of the things you have to do to build a career here. That's a very tough decision to make. When Joel came to LA he did everything correctly.

(Joel McHale) I quit Almost Live! and went back to graduate school for acting because I felt I needed to become a better actor. At Almost Live! I knew I wasn't the best performer or the funniest person but as far as ambition went I knew I had that.

I was an intern in '94, got a job on the show in '95, and then did both graduate school and performing on Almost Live! in '97 and then I completely left it in '98.

(Bob Nelson) You don't see too many people leave a TV show to go back and train themselves. And when he came to LA he worked in theater, he was in TV commercials, he went to drama classes, he went to auditions, he did everything by the book so to look at Joel McHale and say, that's guaranteed that he'd be where he is isn't necessarily so.

(Lauren Weedman) He knew what he wanted and he was so completely focused on it. His energy was so good and positive.

(John Keister) He had a vision and he carried through with it.

(Joel McHale) As fun and great as Almost Live! was I knew that the big game was in Los Angeles. I don't know what I would have done if I stayed in Seattle. I'd just gotten married and I gave myself five years to get work and if it didn't work out I can at least say I tried. It took three and a half years before I landed The Soup. When I first got to LA I could not get a legit agent; all I could get was a commercial agent. I was dropped by my first agency. I got very lucky when I first arrived in LA and got a guest star on Will and Grace and I had no agent at that point. I got an agent out of that and then that agent dropped me about six or eight months later because I wasn't producing for them. They literally said, "Once he's more famous he can come back. This agency is too big for him." They said, "Come back in four years."

(Lauren Weedman) I remember him telling me that he saw Sidney Pollock eating somewhere, and that's normally the kind of guy you don't bother, leave those folks alone who are bothered all the time, but Joel walked right up and charmed him and got some advice from him. I knew that he was so freaking charming, he immediately makes you feel like he's your big brother.

(Joel McHale) That's not exactly what happened. I was on that Will and Grace, right? And Sydney Pollack played Will's father, Eric McCormack's father, and I was in the same show and me not knowing how things worked at that point, I said, "Oh, hey, you're Sydney Pollack, can we go have dinner?" And he agreed. He was like, "Sure." He couldn't have been friendlier. And we talked mostly about Stanley Kubrick. And so it wasn't like I saw him on the street and said, "Hey, let's go to dinner!"

(Lauren Weedman) [Almost Live!] gave me such an opportunity; it gave me a chance to start writing stuff and because of the work I did on Almost Live! that I got the job on the Daily Show. I wasn't aware of how lucky I was to be on Almost Live!, I was young and thought I was too cool for school working on my theater shows. I didn't realize how being on that show changed the course of everything for me. I didn't realize what an institution it was since I didn't grow up there. I learned a ton.

Oh yea, I remember that sketch!

- **What stupid thing will Dale Ellis do next?**
  The game show where contestants try to guess what ridiculous situation the Seattle Supersonic player will inevitably get himself into. Dale did have the knack.

- **Green Riverdance**
  In the tradition of the Irish masterwork, The Riverdance, comes a celebration of the rich culture from the banks of the mighty river that runs through the heart of south King County. Witness...The Kegger Dance, Gotta Pee Dervish, and the Perm Prance.

- **Unsolved Mysteries of Seattle**
  Consider strange cases, such as The woman who really likes all the new area codes, or, What strange force compels local drivers to travel 45 miles per hour when it's dry, 65 when it's raining and 85 when it snows?

1999

- Lance Armstrong wins his first Tour de France.
- Barbie turns 40. Botox sold separately.
- People freak out about Y2K, fearing worldwide computer crashes.
- Safeco Field, new home to the Mariners opens.
- WTO riots in downtown Seattle.
- Almost Live! canceled. All of Seattle wears black. I'm kidding.

This is the End

The show had defied the odds and run for fifteen years, but nothing lasts forever, except maybe the Simpsons. But as I'm writing this, 17 years after Almost Live! was cancelled, the show is still on the air in reruns. It hasn't left the air in 32 years. Even the Simpson's can't claim that. Yet.

(Bob Nelson) The thought that we could be cancelled was always a possibility. When the station was sold to Providence-Journal, that made you worry, and then to Belo, which is a huge corporation, and when a corporation that big owns you you know there's no one in management invested in the show, and you can be cancelled at any time for any reason. As each season ended you would wait and see if you were going to work during the summer, shooting stuff for the next season.

(Bill Stainton) It was getting increasingly more difficult, because those stereotypes that were our bread and butter were no longer accurate, so it was harder and harder to write stuff that was fresh.

We ended up writing the same jokes, the same sketches over and over again with different veneers on them.

(Ed Wyatt) Near the end I was frustrated with a lot of things. I wasn't making a lot of money, I thought the show had gone about as far as it could go, I thought we were recycling the same stuff until Joel and those guys came in and gave it a freshen up.

(Nancy Guppy) I think the show for me was ending for three years. I probably should have left earlier; I didn't have anything to say anymore. Everything has a life span. I think in the last couple of years there was a little bit of phoning it in, speaking for myself. When it was cancelled I did not have a regret at all.

(Tracey Conway) I think that most things have an arc of four or five years and yet it was our livelihood you know, that was our job and it's hard to walk away from something when you're doing it as your job. So I think...I probably should have gracefully got out and found something to do by '97 or so. You know I wish I had been braver and had jumped, but it's pretty hard to climb out of a very comfortable satisfying job just because, well, I'm getting a little long in the tooth.

(Bill Stainton) For about five years straight Pat Cashman would ask me to have lunch with him during the summer break and he would say, "I just don't think I can do this anymore," and then he'd always come back. But after season 15, during that break, we had lunch and he said, "That's it, I'm not going to be part of the show anymore." He was our go-to guy, he was a very prolific writer, we're all in our forties now, it was getting harder and harder to write fresh jokes, and for me it was a combination of all of those things. When Cashman told me that he was done I kind of thought that was it.

(Nancy Guppy) I think Cashman leaving, I think that was an excuse for them to go, "You know what, let's deep six this thing and not spend this money." At that time TV stations were still printing money. They were just not printing it as fast as they used to.

(Steve Wilson) Pat actually announced that he was leaving the show, he was not coming back. He was doing his morning radio show which means he had to be up around four in the morning every single day. And then on Saturdays he would be here from, like, eight in the morning until midnight, which left him one day, Sunday to re-coup. I would imagine his wife was ready to shoot him in the head.

(Pat Cashman) I don't know…I mean, I realized that I wanted to leave the show. I did feel like the oldest person that's in the cast, and I just felt like I really got to get some younger blood in here. I really kind of loved the idea, that what I would like to do is be the mentor or overseer with some other, younger people around, and help them learn to write and that sort of thing.

(Bill Stainton) My hope always had been, probably from the third or fourth year of doing the show, that I would turn the keys over to somebody else. There was always that hope that it would just continue.

(John Keister) We got to a point where we'd gotten old enough that there were certain roles that we couldn't really convincingly play and I knew [the end] was coming at some point.

(Jay Cascio) You could never see the end of the show in the quality of the program. The numbers and ratings were really good, so the normal indicators weren't there. The indicators were the economy. The economy was falling apart. At the time we were owned by Belo and it was really just a matter of looking at the landscape in front of us. Trying to determine if we would be able to fund it. Because even though it had the numbers the time period was very hard to make money in. It was my recommendation to cancel the show and the Station Manager, Dennis Williamson's decision. I made the decision looking at where the program was and looking at where it was going. Not only was the economic horizon very foggy and very uncertain but I think one of the greatest minds behind Almost Live! was Pat Cashman, and Pat at that point was looking to do something different. I had to look at the next year of Almost Live! without Pat and when I looked at how that program ran and where a lot of the creative juice and the excitement and the passion and the motivation and that determination and everything else, a lot of it came from Pat. In my years we were cycling a lot of freelance people through on the show and it was working. Lauren Weedman, of course, Joel McHale. But I think the point we were looking at from a financial standpoint and thinking, How can we support Almost Live!? Will we be able to support Almost Live! at the same level that we currently are? And they'll be the first to tell you that we hardly supported them at all. They were amazing at what they were able to do with as little as they had.

(Bill Stainton) It really was a two-bit show, they spent very little money on it and virtually no marketing on it which always pissed us off.

(Ross Shafer) Oh my god, did they spend any money on the show? I never heard.

(Bob Nelson) The only frustrating part was that we knew we were doing it on a budget that no one else, even on a cable show, would have to put up with.

(Jay Cascio) When I pulled the plug the reaction was very interesting. We didn't make the decision on the fly but it wasn't something we belabored over for a long time because it was fairly obvious. When you've got a product that is so good but you know that you may not be able to sustain the level of quality and at the same time you don't think you'll have the funding to support it, my decision was to take them out on top. If I were them I wouldn't want to be put through what could have possibly happened over the next couple of years, when you take away what little money they have. It was a painful decision but it was the right decision. I never second-guessed it whatsoever.

(John Keister) I met with Jay and tried to convince him that, of course, the cast had aged out, but the show was still a really important part of the community, and why not bring in some younger actors—you wouldn't have to pay them as much—and you'd still have this show that had created such good will in the community. And his response was, "What's Almost Live! without Pat?"

There was a long uncomfortable silence and I excused myself from his office. But before I left I asked him, "When will the final show air?" And he informed me that they would not be taking Almost Live! off the air, and now it has aired in reruns longer than the original production. The cast doesn't earn a dime from these reruns but in my conversations with everyone on the cast the feeling is that they'd rather have it on the air than not.

(Bob Nelson) We didn't have a real warning when it happened. We did work through the summer in '99, and once they pay ten people to work from June through September you feel you're doing one more season. So it was actually kind of a shock when we were cancelled.

(Steve Wilson) We were shocked. They gave absolutely no indication that there would not be a 16th season. We already had 13 or 14 bits in the can from over the summer. The reason it was cancelled was that show didn't make enough money, which was BS; it was all BS.

(John Keister) [They said] that the business model didn't work, the business model just doesn't work on the show. Yeah, right. Give me a break.

(Bill Stainton) The one thing that ticked me off was why KING said they cancelled the show, which was that it wasn't making money, and that's crap. I was the Executive Producer; I was privy to the financials. The show was making money. Somebody in the sales department told me, "Even if the show was just breaking even you keep it on the air because it's one of these little crown jewels, it's something nobody else has." But we were now owned by Belo, which was based in Dallas, and we were just a line item on a budget.

(Erik Lacitis) I don't know what the finances were. If I had been them I would have kept the show going as long as it was breaking even. Even if it was making minimal amount of money the goodwill that it would generate KING 5 was tremendous.

(Jeff Renner) We were very sorry to see the show cancelled; we thought it fit a nice niche in the Seattle area. I think it was a poor decision to cancel it. It was still doing pretty well in the ratings, but I think it was one of those things that really spoke to the unique character of Seattle and it was an opportunity for us to break out of the mold and say, "We're going to program to that character in Seattle and do something a little different and a little fun."

(John Keister) I never felt we got the straight story, I am pretty convinced that the reason we were fired was because Dennis Williamson, who was the General Manager, was at that time, we didn't know he was auditioning for a job at the BELO head office in Dallas. Whatever he was auditioning for, he was cutting costs all over KING to prove that he was a really lean and mean financial guy. Then in that first kind of ill-fated Internet boom the TV stations thought they were going to make just unbelievable amounts of money by combining, you could sell ads on TV and the Internet as well. They had all these ridiculous pipe dreams of how much money they were going to make, but in order to do that you had to do have an Internet division and there was a hiring freeze, so they had to get rid of somebody in order to hire people to do the Internet and I always felt that's why they pulled the plug on the show, so they could move us out and could move the Internet people in. I don't think anyone will ever know the real story but I think that's the real story, what they told us was complete BS.

(Steve Wilson) We were owned by Belo and at that time the Internet was taking off and everyone was saying, "You gotta have a website, you gotta have a website." And back in '99 in order to have a website you had to bring on your own staff; you needed to have the wherewithal to do it yourself. So Belo basically said, "What's this group of nine people there that are full-time benefitted? Well get rid of them, we gotta get a website up because that's gonna be the future." They decided that we were done and that the website was going to make them money. And it wasn't long after that that they did hire nine people to construct a website and they kept them on for, like, five months and got rid of them all and outsourced it immediately. The thing was, the show made a 23% return on investment, and they said, "Well, you gotta bring in 26 or we're going to cancel the show." Now, if you can imagine anything getting a 23% return on investment today...you're lucky if can get 3%. It was just a matter of warm bodies, they had to eliminate warm bodies, and they were a news organization, Belo was a newspaper and they didn't do entertainment stuff. This show was just foreign to them. Now, the show brought in at least a million dollars every year but they didn't care. They thought we really need to get into the Internet thing.

(Jay Cascio) So far as I know, Almost Live!'s cancellation had nothing to do with KING's website. I don't remember the year, but I contracted with an outside company to develop the original

KING website. Shortly after, KING hired Internet sales people and content managers but the website was, for the most part, run from our corporate offices in Dallas. All of the Belo websites became uniform. We worked hard to find a title sponsor for Almost Live! because we couldn't sell spot ads (in that time period) for enough money to support the show.

(Steve Wilson) The people who were really shocked were the sales people, because they could sell this show; they made so much money off it. Tons of money. And they were like, "What? No!" But the edict had already been sent down. So they basically dismantled it.

(Feliks Banel) It's weird that the show lasted that long. It's like something went wrong in a good way to make it last that long. Because local TV is so cynical, especially under out of town ownership, it beat the odds. It's bizarre how long Almost Live! survived. They got away with it.

(Hans-Eric Gosch) We were a family who actually got paid to play dress up, make each other laugh and throw dummies off rooftops. We also knew we were damn lucky to be doing what we were doing and that it wouldn't last forever.

(John Keister) It was the best job I ever had, particularly when you compare it to the rest of show business. In show business you never know who your friends are, good ideas are ruined for the dumbest reasons, most people you work for have no idea what they're doing, money is the primary focus.

At Almost Live! we were good friends, there was very little competitiveness, the best ideas always made their way into the show, and I couldn't wait to unleash it all on the audience every week. There's never been another work situation that's come close. Definitely the best years of my life.

Other names that were kicked around

- Seattle Review
- Positively Seattle
- The Before the Rest of the Week Show
- Seattle at Large
- Seattle on the Half Shell (Seriously?)
- The Comedy Zone
- Laughing Zone
- Funny Business
- The Ad Lib
- Comic Relief
- Night Life
- The City Tonight
- Show Biz Seattle
- Night Off
- Comedy Tonight
- Good Stuff
- Almost Hollywood
- Funny Pages
- After Dark
- Laughing Pad
- Free TV
- Take Five
- The Night Club
- Spotlight Seattle
- Only Kidding
- Appearing Nightly
- On the Air
- Technical Difficulty

Almost Live

	KING 5's Almost Live! Ballard Driving Academy TIME: 2:24
VIDEO	**AUDIO**
	(Polka music under) (Announcer) And now a special announcement from the Ballard Driving Academy, here's Ole Torgerson.
Ole Torgerson—John Keister—standing by car. John in car with student—Bob Nelson. Bob opens the door, hangs the seat belt	(Ole—John Keister) Here at the Ballard Driving Academy for over 35 years we've been teaching people to drive just like they live in Ballard. Welcome to the Ballard Driving Academy. (Student) Thank you. (John) Now before we start please adjust

out the door and slams the door so the belt is dragging on the pavement. The car drives away with the seat belt dragging.	your seatbelt. (John) Okay, good. Ah, now check your left turn signal. Okay, now leave that on all day. Make sure that never goes off. All right? Everything seems to check out, now let's go into traffic.
John and Bob in car driving along. John looks back. A line of cars are lined up behind	(John) Whoa, where's the fire? How fast are you going? (Student—Bob) Uh, ten. (John) Bring it down to seven, there you go. That's as fast as we go in Ballard. Now let me see how many cars you're holding up. Six...seven...eight. All

with angry drivers.	right, eight cars, you passed.
Shot of the car on the street. John and Bob in car. Car weaving all over road.	(John) You're not using the whole road. (Bob) What? (John) You pay taxes on the whole road don't you? (John) Yea? (John) Well use the whole road. Weave. There you go. Weave. (Bob) Keep it to seven miles an hour, just weave, yea. Switch lanes at random. Don't let them see what you're doing. That's it; just keep weaving. That's good.
John and Bob in car.	(John) How long you lived in Ballard? (Bob) All my life? (John) How long you want to live here?

John nods approvingly.	(Student) Till I die. (John) All right.
Car driving down street. John and Bob in car as Bob tries parallel parking. Car hits car behind with a loud crunch. Car hits car in front with a loud crunch.	(John) Now pull over here and let's try some parallel parking. (John) Now don't look back. Do it by sound. (Bob) What do you mean? (John) By sound. (John) Okay, that's far enough; now pull forward. Don't look. (John) There. Perfect. Good. That's the Ballard way. That's good.
Text on screen.	(Announcer) At the Ballard Driving Academy you'll also learn these useful skills. Using curbs to steer. Getting stuck on median dividers. New looks in hats. How

	to argue with paramedics. Stopping 20 feet before the intersection then lurching forward. Turning right, no left, no, wait a minute. Stop!
John outside the car with the student. John slaps an Uff Da! sticker on the back of the car. John turns to the camera.	(John) Bob, you passed all your tests, so you've earned the sticker. (John) Keep it on your car at all times. It means you're a Ballard driver. Congratulations. (Student) Thank you. (John) Wouldn't you like to be a Ballard driver too? Come see us today.

Almost Live

	KING 5's Almost Live! Roscoe's Oriental Rug Emporium TIME: 1:54

VIDEO	**AUDIO**
Pat Cashman in front of Oriental rugs. His read begins low key but as he goes along he gets louder and more demonstrative until he's screaming at the top of his lungs. Text on screen reflecting what he's saying, almost verbatim.	(Pat) At Roscoe's Oriental Rug Emporium we're saying goodbye. We're closing our store forever, and you can save like never before. Roscoe's Oriental Rug Emporium is saying That's it. It's over. We're done. Time's up. Farewell. So long. Tootleloo. We're outta here. We really mean It. No kidding. This is really it this time. I know we've said it before but this is the real deal

this time. We're hittin' the bricks. Gonna mosey. Gonna sashay. Gonna clear out. Vamoos. Saying adios. Ciao. Auf Wiedersehen. Sayonara. Au Revoir. Hasta luego. Godspeed until we meet again, which we won't, because Roscoe's Oriental Rug Emporium is closing forever. We're never coming back. It's over. We're done. We're shoving off, bowing out, flaking off, getting done. It's at an end. We're cutting out. Kaput. Finished. Drop the curtain. Break camp. Pull up stakes. Finis. This is absolutely, positively it this time. We're not pulling your leg on this. Roscoe's Oriental Rug Emporium is down the road. We swear we won't ever be back. It ain't gonna happen. Forget about it. We're shutting it down. We've lost our lease. Can't find it. Don't care, cuz we're done. Closing shop. Putting up the Shutters. Bolting the doors. Slamming them closed. Gonna board the place up. Nailing it shut. Big nails. Nothing gets in or out. Sealing it off. We're history. We really, really, really, really mean it this time. We're not jerking your chain on this. This ain't no snow job. We're not bluffing. No kidding. So shag your big fat bottom down here, PDQ, cuz I swear if you dawdle or dink around you'll be SOL, cuz we're closing forever. Any day now, could be a matter of weeks, days, maybe tomorrow. But then, that's it.

Roscoe's Oriental Rug Emporium, going out of business since 1957.

	KING 5's Almost Live! Billy Quan—Yard Sale of Fury TIME: 2:08
VIDEO	**AUDIO**
Text on screen: Mind your manners with Billy Quan	(Announcer with bad Japanese accent) It's time for Mind your Manners with Billy Quan. Today's episode: Yard Sale of Fury.
Billy in front of his house having a yard sale. Steve Wilson picks up a mug.	(Billy voice over— Pat Cashman's voice) I've got some very nice stuff here. This ought to go very well today. (Customer 1—Steve Wilson in a high whiny badly dubbed voice) Hey, how much you want for this mug?

Billy uses very exaggerated arm motions as he speaks. His mouth is totally out of synch with the audio—like a bad 1970s Japanese martial arts movie.	(Billy) That is a fine piece going back to the Ming Dynasty. (Steve) Uhhhh, I've give you a quarter for it. (Billy) Fair enough. (Steve) Here you go. (Billy) Have a nice day.
Billy sees John Keister rummaging through some records. John picks up a record—Kiss—Love Gun. The record flies out of the jacket and into the	(Billy) Oh! (John Keister in a badly dubbed voice) What a bunch of worthless crap. (Billy) Well for your information these are valuable collectibles. (John) How much you want for this? Whoops.

street where it is run over by a passing car.	(Billy) (Screams)
	(John) Huh?
	(Billy) You idiot, that was Love Gun by Kiss. That's a classic album!
John picks up several more records and begins throwing them at Billy like they're throwing stars.	(John) Oh, you want albums, huh? Try these! Ha!
	(Billy) Uh oh.
Billy holds up Peter Frampton's Frampton Comes Alive album jacket to block the flying records. John throws one last record in slow motion.	(Billy) Frampton Come Alive!
Billy catches it, spins the record on his finger and uses his fingernail as a	(KC) Shake, shake, shake. Shake, shake, shake. Shake your booty. Shake your

needle plays KC and Sunshine Band's Shake Your Booty.

booty.

John begins to dance.

(John) Arrrr!

John stops and picks up a giant wooden spoon.

(Billy) He is most impressive with his utensil.

Billy picks up a giant wooden fork. John spins the spoon like a Bo stick or Nun-chucks. John attacks Billy with the spoon but Billy counters by jabbing John in the groin with the fork. He pitches John over his shoulder. John jumps on a bike and rides away.

(Billy) Stop, you

Billy does a flying kick. He flies, and flies, slowly catching up to John on the bike until John takes a corner and crashes down a long staircase. Billy stands over John's body and speaks to the camera.	have not paid for that. Jerk. Ahhhhhhhhhhhhhhhhhh. (Billy) Remember boys and girls, be a courteous shopper or Billy will junk you.
	(Announcer) Remember kids, be like Billy. Behave yourself.

Almost Live

VIDEO	AUDIO
	KING 5's Almost Live! COPS in Kent TIME: 4:56
Rolling text on screen.	(Announcer) Due to the graphic nature of the following program there may be certain scenes that are not suitable for some members of our viewing audience...like wusses, little wimps and weenies.
Video clips of people getting tackled by cops, police lights, etc.	(Music up) Bad boys, bad boys, whatcha gonna do, whatcha gonna do when they come for you?
Graphic: COPS in Kent	(Announcer) COPS. In Kent.
Driver's perspective. Driving	(Cop—John Keister) Monday is always a

by Chain Saw Bob's. Welcome to Kent sign. Gun Sport. People walking by.	little bit tense around Kent because, you know, tonight is women's mud wrestling night and everyone's a little anxious for work. Sometimes a little too anxious if you know what I mean.
Sgt. Verne Ramsey (John Keister) in car.	(Radio) Car 25 we have a possible 124 at Cloudy and James. (John) Uh, yea this is car 25, roger, be there in a second.
Two guys pushing each other on the side of the road. John approaches on foot.	(John) Yea, we've got some big problems here. Excuse me gentlemen, excuse me, where are your caps? (Guy 1—Bob Nelson) What do you mean? (John) Do you realize that while you are

within the city limits of Kent all males under 35 years of age must be wearing caps?

(Guy 2—Ed Wyatt) We forgot em at home.

(John) You forgot em at home. All right, well I've got some stand by caps, I want you to put these on until you can get down to the Minute Mart. You can wear a 'Damn I'm good', a 'Honk if you're horny' or even just a Caterpillar hat, anything like that, but you must be wearing a cap as long as you're…Hey, hey, c'mere buddy. What's the matter with you?

Ed Wyatt makes a break for it. John

grabs him. Tracey Conway walks up to Ed with a paper bag.	Look, I don't write these laws, I gotta enforce them. (Woman—Tracey Conway) I, I got beer, and generic was okay, right? (Bob) Great, yea! (Woman) Okay.
John confronts the woman.	(John) What do we have here? Excuse me young lady; do you know where you are? (Woman) Kent? (John) That's right, and do you realize that you're in violation of the Kent big hair ordinance? Look, all women in Kent have to have
John takes out a tape measure and measures the woman's	their hair teased out at least 20 inches. Oh, honey, you're way

hair from side to side.	under! You're way under! Ah, I'm gonna let you go this time but you've gotta get this teased out, okay? Now make it big, okay? All right.
John yells at Ed to get his cap on.	I'm gonna give you guys a warning this time...Get your cap on! Get it on!
	I'm gonna give you a warning this time but I want you to stay out of trouble. If you can't stay out of trouble you stay out of Kent. Am I clear?
	(Guys) Yes, yes sir.
John walking away, speaking to the camera, shaking his head.	(John) All right.
	(John) In Kent with no caps. (sigh)
John in patrol car.	(John) People in

Two people walking past Cave Man Kitchen.	Kent, they're, you know they're basically good people but, whoa, what's that over there? What have we got here? What have we got here?
John out of car chasing men—Steve Wilson and Bill Nye.	(John) Hey, hey, now listen I want to see your driver's licenses and both of your Boeing IDs. (Guy--Bill) We don't have Boeing IDs, we don't work at Boeing. (Guy--Steve) We work downtown. (John) Well I guess that's pretty obvious isn't it? (pause) You're north enders aren't you? You are! I saw you walk right

past the Cave Man Kitchen. Now everybody knows the only reason north enders come to Kent is to come to the Cave Man Kitchen. You didn't stop there; you're acting very suspicious. I want to know what's going on and I want to know now!

(Steve) Okay, we came down to laugh at hicks.

(John) To laugh at hicks. Very nice gentlemen, very nice. All right, I'm afraid I'm going to have to escort you back to I-5.

(Bill) Okay, actually thank you officer,

The guys look embarrassed.

	it's pretty scary around here.
	(Steve) Yea, can I have a latte please?
	(John) No! Get out of here.
Driver's perspective—Driving by the Kent city hall.

Driving by Long septic tank company. | (John) Oh, there's the Kent city hall. Boy that's a beautiful building. I get chills every time I look at it. You know Kent is a beautiful city. Of course, maybe it just seems that way, stuck between Renton and Auburn as it is. I think it's beautiful.

(Radio) Car 25, a domestic at the Semi-Scenic apartments.

(John) Uh, roger, roger, I'll be right |

	there.
John rushes into apartment where a man and woman are arguing. The man's sitting on a couch with a beer.	(John) Hey, hold it down, hold it down. What's going on here? (Man—Bill Stainton) I didn't do anything. (Woman) He changed the channel of Matlock.
John pulls a gun on the man.	(John) What?!! Hold it. That's a very serious crime in Kent. You never change the channel off of Matlock! Why would you do something like that? (Bill) Well I wanted to watch the Bill Moyer special on channel 9, c'mon, he was great in Stripes. (John) No, no you're thinking of Bill

	Murray. It was Bill Murray in Stripes. Bill Moyer is the guy who talks to intelligent people about meaningful subjects on channel 9.
	(Bill) Honey, change it back to Matlock.
John drags the man off the couch.	(John) No, no it's too late for that. Get up. I'm gonna read you your rights. Now listen to me very carefully; you got the right to remain silent (pause) although you can talk about the 64 funny cars that are gonna be at SIR this weekend, okay? All right, uh, if you need a lawyer...well

John pulls out a tape measure and measures the woman's hair. He seems satisfied.	we'll go up to Bellevue and get you one. All right, you understand that? Now stay right here, I need to check something. Okay.
	(Music) Bad boys, bad boys, whatcha gonna do. Whatcha gonna do when they come for you?
	(Announcer) COPS in Kent.

Almost Live

VIDEO	AUDIO
	KING 5's Almost Live! Date with an Engineer TIME: 2:15
Text on screen.	(Sinister, high tension music under) (Announcer) She thought she was going on a dream date...
Woman on phone— Tracey Conway— sitting on couch, holding a newspaper.	(Woman--Tracey) Yes, I'm excited. He says in his ad that he's a professional man, so that, I dunno, I'm hoping that he's a lawyer or a doctor or something.
Text on screen.	(Announcer) But soon she'll live through every woman's nightmare.
Woman on phone. Very excited.	(Doorbell rings) (Woman) Oh my god,

She hangs up.	he's here. I'll call you later, all right, I will, bye!
The woman answers the door. Her eyes jump to his polyester tie tucked into his shirt. Pocket protector. Tape on the glasses. The woman grabs her head and screams.	(Woman) (Screams)
Horror movie text over Bill Nye standing at door holding daisies.	(Announcer) Date…with an engineer.
Text on screen.	(Announcer) You'll experience horror beyond belief at…an engineer's party!
A group of nerdy engineers—Bob Nelson, John Keister—giggling	

with their calculators. The woman walks in with Bill Nye.	(Bill) Guys, this is Tracey.
John and the other engineers begin madly tapping away on their calculators. John holds out his calculator just before the other engineers. He looks immensely proud. One of the other engineers—Bob Nelson—makes his ears pointy. John points to Tracey.	(John) Oh great you made it! We're just about done. Ready guys? Go! (Bill) Cool. (John) First! (Bill) Oh no way! Whoa, guys! Is the popcorn ready? (John) Almost. And then we're gonna play Star Trek. Look, he's Spock. (Bill) Cool! (John) Hey, she could play Nurse Chapel. C'mon, beam up, it'll be fun.
Transition to Bill	(Bill) See you guys!

and Tracey leaving the party.	Bye! (Bill) God, those guys crack me up. I love working at Boeing.
Text on screen.	(Announcer) You'll writhe in agony as you witness…an engineer at dinner.
Bill and Tracey at dinner. Bill's typing on his 1990s computer at the table.	(Bill) So, I've worked the data on my computer, I've got it on floppy, and if it goes well I think I can transfer over to hard disc. (Waiter—Ed Wyatt) Here's your bill. (Bill) Oh thanks, thanks. Uh, whenever I tip I like to use a little formula, it's kinda neat. Let me show you how it goes. You take the quality

	of the service…
Text on screen.	(Announcer) You'll feel heart-stopping amazement when…an engineer tries to score.
Bill and Tracey at Tracey's front door. Bill takes some condoms out of his shirt pocket. He uses the tester. Tracey slowly closes the door on him.	(Tracey) Hey, it was really interesting. (Bill) Can I come in? I bought some of these. They're latex. We can test them. I always carry a tester on my belt to make sure they're okay. Yea, we're in business! This one's fine. This one's fine. How many do you think we're gonna need?
Text on screen.	(Announcer) Date…with an engineer!

Almost Live

	KING 5's Almost Live! Folk Songs of South King County TIME: 2:12
VIDEO	**AUDIO**
Transition to beauty shot of Mt. Rainier. Shots from each of the listed communities.	(Announcer—Pat Cashman) South King County. A land of enchantment. From Renton to Auburn. From Burien to Black Diamond. It's been celebrated in song ever since man put really huge tires on a perfectly good pick up.
Album cover. Two singers—Bill Stainton and Bob Nelson—sit on stools strumming guitars in a studio.	(Singer—Bob Nelson—singing) *Sorry Honey but your hair's too big for my truck. I can only haul a half a ton in my truck.* (Announcer) Now you can get all your

Song titles on screen.	favorite songs about this very special place on just one album. Folk songs of South King County. As performed by Riley and Nelson. You get all your favorites. (Bob—singing) *Good old fashioned...Sea-Tac massage.* (Bob—singing) *Honey come quick, I've got an itch. Got an itch.* (Announcer) You'll thrill to the tales of life as it's lived in South King County. (Bob—singing) *Yell if you see the cops a-comin', uh huh.* (Bob—singing) *Everybody...get a couple bucks. Cuz*

it's keggggggger…kegger in the field.

(Announcer) You'll be moved by the songs of love for the places you remember so well.

(Bob—singing) *Have you ever seen Kent in the moonlight? It can really bring a tear to your eye.*

(Announcer) You'll also get the classics, updated for that South King County state of mind. Like, Kisses sweeter than Schlitz. On top of a gravel pit. And everybody's favorite…

(Bob—singing) *I'm going to sit right down and drink beer 'til I pass out.*

	Tomorrow I'll do it again. (Announcer) Folk Songs of South King County. Also available in 8-track.

	KING 5's Almost Live! Speed Walker—Kingdome Bomber TIME: 3:47
VIDEO	**AUDIO**
Reporter Jeff Bimmel—Bill Nye—walks toward the Kingdome.	(Voice Over—Bill Nye) Jeff Bimmel, reporter for the Daily Dealer. Today's assignment: King Dogs. It started out as a routine story. But then!
Cutaway to a bomb being placed on the Kingdome football goal posts.	
A radio at the security desk in the Kingdome. The security guard freaks out.	(Radio) Attention citizens of Seattle. I'm gonna blow up the Kingdome with a big bomb! Ah-ha-ha-ha-ha! (Guard) A bomb!

Reporter Jeff Bimmel—Bill Nye— walks up with his notebook and pad in hand.	Quick, call the Mayor, call the Chief of Security, call anybody, we need some help, please help us, call the state patrol! Call the police!
Bill runs into a Kingdome ticket office and instantly emerges dressed as the superhero Speed Walker.	(Bill) This looks like a job for… …Speed Walker!
Bill as Speed Walker walks briskly down a sidewalk.	(Announcer) Yes, it's Speed Walker. The physically fit super hero who fights crime while maintaining strict adherence to the regulations of the International

	Speed Walking Association. Heel, toe, heel, toe. Speed Walker!
Bill walks onto the Kingdome football field. He spots someone placing something on the opposite end zone goal posts. He speed walks to confront the man—Ed Wyatt. The man runs away. Bill checks the bomb's clock. He's got 15 minutes. He sets his watch and pursues the man up the Kingdome ramps in perfect speed walking form. Ed hides behind a pillar.	(Bill) I've lost him. I need more time.

Bill stops and checks his watch. He turns and speed walks down the ramps.	
Bill goes back to the bomb and dials the minute hand back to 15 minutes again.	
He spots the bomber on the 300 level.	
Bill confronts Ed in the bleachers. Ed is out of breath.	(Bill) May I see your ticket stub? Punk?
Bill drags Ed out on the 300 level outdoor landing and holds him against the railing by his coat labels.	
Ed look terrified. Bill looks psychotic.	(Ed) Who are you? (Bill) I'm Speed Walker.
Bill tosses Ed over	

the railing. As the body falls Bill speed walks down the ramps and catches the falling Ed.	
Cut to the security guard at the security office. Bill hands Ed over to the guard.	(Guard) Yes Chief… (Bill) Officer, here's someone I think you'd like to meet. It's your gridiron culprit. (Guard) Thanks Speed Walker. (To Ed) You're under arrest. (Bill) I've got a bomb to take care of. (Guard) Thanks again, Speed Walker.
Cut away to the bomb. Bill picks it up and speed walks away.	
Cut away to a line of lockers: Speed	

Walker Shoe locker. Jersey locker. Cape locker. Bomb locker. Bill slaps a piece of tape on the bomb's clock's second hand and stuffs it in the locker.	(Bill) That should hold it for a while.
Cut back to the security guard office. Mild mannered reporter Jeff Bimmel walks up. Speed Walker logo flies in.	(Bill) What happened officer? (Guard) We had a bomb in the Kingdome, but Speed Walker saved the day. (Bill) I'm Jeff Bimmel of the Daily Dealer, tell me all about it. (Guard) You should have seen Speed Walker, he come roaring in here, he took care of the problem...(fade out)

	KING 5's Almost Live! Trivial Pursuit WSU Edition TIME: 1:10
VIDEO	**AUDIO**
Smug looking man asking question off of card. Ed Wyatt looking puzzled.	(Classical music under) (Smug man) Who was the title character in the Merchant of Venice? (Ed Wyatt) I don't know. (Smug man) Antonio. Sheesh. (Announcer) Do you find regular Trivial Pursuit way too hard? (Music change—Hard rock)
Group of 4 Cougs playing. Two Cougs playing, toasting paper cups	(Announcer) Then try the WSU version. You'll have hours of fun playing in

before chugging them. Drunk Coug—Steve Wilson—filling paper cup from a keg.	categories like Beer. Sex. Cars. Sex in cars after beer. And Idaho.
Steve asking question off a card.	(Steve Wilson) A woman who will go to bed with you after one beer is called a… (John Keiser) A Gamma Phi! (Steve) Correct!
Game pieces moved around board. John asking question off a card. Ed looking confident. Drunk Coug—Steve—trying to still fill his paper cup from a keg.	(John) A guy who can drink six pitchers of beer without passing out is a… (Ed) Designated driver.
Ed asking question off a card.	(Ed) What's the best serving temperature for beer?

	(Bob Nelson) Doesn't matter. (Ed) That's right.
Drunk Coug—Steve—drinking straight from the keg tap. Steve asking question off a card.	(Announcer) Finally, questions you can answer. (Steve) Which is worse to barf up? Popcorn, pizza or Doritos?
Trivial Pursuit box with Coug logo.	(Announcer) Trivial Pursuit. From Wazzu to you!

Almost Live

Almost Live

33879745R00167

Made in the USA
Middletown, DE
31 July 2016